Access to History

This book is to be returned on or before
the last date stamped below.

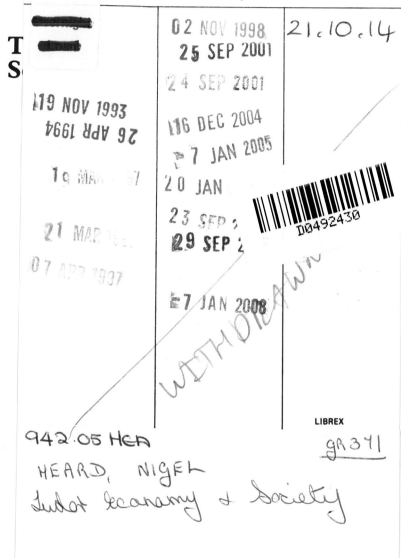

Access to History

General Editor: Keith Randell

Tudor Economy and Society

Nigel Heard

Hodder & Stoughton

LONDON SYDNEY AUCKLAND

The cover illustration shows a scene from 'The Life and Death of Henry Unton', c.1596, artist unknown (courtesy National Portrait Gallery, London).

Some other titles in the series:

Henry VII
Caroline Rogers
ISBN 0 340 53801 5

Henry VIII and the Government of England
Keith Randell
ISBN 0 340 55325 1

Henry VIII and the Reformation in England
Keith Randell
ISBN 0 340 57805 X

Edward VI and Mary: A Mid-Tudor Crisis?
Nigel Heard
ISBN 0 340 53560 1

Charles V: Ruler, Dynast and Defender of the Faith 1500–58
Stewart MacDonald
ISBN 0 340 53558 X

From Revolt to Independence: The Netherlands 1550–1650
Martyn Rady
ISBN 0 340 51803 0

British Library Cataloguing in Publication Data
Heard, Nigel
Tudor Economy and Society. – (Access to History Series)
I. Title II. Series
942.05

ISBN 0 340 55519 X

First published 1992

Typeset by Wearset, Boldon, Tyne and Wear
Printed in Great Britain for the educational publishing division of Hodder & Stoughton Ltd, Mill Road, Dunton Green, Sevenoaks, Kent by Page Bros (Norwich) Ltd

Contents

Preface

To the general reader

Although the *Access to History* series has been designed with the needs of students studying the subject at higher examination levels very much in mind, it also has a great deal to offer the general reader. The main body of the text (i.e. ignoring the Study Guides at the ends of chapters) forms a readable and yet stimulating survey of a coherent topic as studied by historians. However, each author's aim has not merely been to provide a clear explanation of what happened in the past (to interest and inform): it has also been assumed that most readers wish to be stimulated into thinking further about the topic and to form opinions of their own about the significance of the events that are described and discussed (to be challenged). Thus, although no prior knowledge of the topic is expected on the reader's part, she or he is treated as an intelligent and thinking person throughout. The author tends to share ideas and possibilities with the reader, rather than passing on numbers of so-called 'historical truths'.

To the student reader

There are many ways in which the series can be used by students studying History at a higher level. It will, therefore, be worthwhile thinking about your own study strategy before you start your work on this book. Obviously, your strategy will vary depending on the aim you have in mind, and the time for study that is available to you.

If, for example, you want to acquire a general overview of the topic in the shortest possible time, the following approach will probably be the most effective:

1 Read chapter 1 and think about its contents.
2 Read the 'Making notes' section at the end of chapter 2 and decide whether it is necessary for you to read this chapter.
3 If it is, read the chapter, stopping at each heading or * to note down the main points that have been made.
4 Repeat stage 2 (and stage 3 where appropriate) for all the other chapters.

If, however, your aim is to gain a thorough grasp of the topic, taking however much time is necessary to do so, you may benefit from carrying out the same procedure with each chapter, as follows:

1 Read the chapter as fast as you can, and preferably at one sitting.
2 Study the flow diagram at the end of the chapter, ensuring that you understand the general 'shape' of what you have just read.

3   Read the 'Making notes' section (and the 'Answering essay questions' section, if there is one) and decide what further work you need to do on the chapter. In particularly important sections of the book, this will involve reading the chapter a second time and stopping at each heading and * to think about (and to write a summary of) what you have just read.

4   Attempt the 'Source-based questions' section. It will sometimes be sufficient to think through your answers, but additional understanding will often be gained by forcing yourself to write them down.

When you have finished the main chapters of the book, study the 'Further Reading' section and decide what additional reading (if any) you will do on the topic.

This book has been designed to help make your studies both enjoyable and successful. If you can think of ways in which this could have been done more effectively, please write to tell me. In the meantime, I hope that you will gain greatly from your study of History.

Keith Randell

CHAPTER 1

Introduction: The Background

1 Social and Economic History

At the end of the nineteenth century a widespread belief in optimism and 'progress' led some leading historians to think that it might be possible to write 'ultimate' history. This, it was hoped, would provide an interpretation of the past that was acceptable to all historians. Just as the First World War destroyed belief in optimism and 'progress', so it ended hopes of consensus among historians. Today all periods of history are areas of controversy and debate; none more so than the social and economic history of sixteenth-century England. It has been suggested that not only is there disagreement among historians as to the answers, but equally about the very questions to be asked. In 1961 a leading twentieth-century philosopher of history, J. Carr, commented that historical facts were like fish on a fishmonger's slab which the historian takes home and then 'cooks and serves in whatever style appeals to him'. Over the last three decades this has become even more the case. Old issues such as the 'rise of the gentry' remain unresolved. New approaches – the history of the family, urban history and latterly women's history – have come into prominence. For the student just beginning to study history this can be very confusing. It is important to remember that each historian is selecting events and 'facts' to substantiate his or her own particular historical interpretation.

    * The ways in which historians interpret social and economic history have changed dramatically during the twentieth century. In the nineteenth century interest was centred on the development of democracy and the nation state. For this reason British historians tended to concentrate on political and constitutional history, and writing biographies of leading political figures. Social and economic history was rarely considered, and even then it was mainly made up of descriptions of the life-style of the ruling elites. Growing social and economic instability in the early part of the twentieth century undermined the confidence characteristic of the late nineteenth century. This led to the recognition that social and economic history had some importance. Economic fears caused by the Great Depression following the First World War focused attention on the process and causes of industrialisation, particularly on the British Industrial Revolution. This so-called 'new history' was taken a stage further by the *Annales* school of historians in France, who hoped to achieve 'total' history. They set out to examine the whole of society in every aspect, and drew upon

See Preface for explanation of * symbol.

other disciplines, such as sociology, geography, psychology and economics, to help widen their insight. However, British social historians concentrated upon investigating social problems, such as poverty, and researching labour and trade union history. These developments, and the increasing tension between Eastern European Marxist and Western capitalist economies, created rising interest in the Marxist theories of history which had been largely ignored by historians in the previous century. This interpretation viewed history in terms of social conflict (class struggle) which would lead eventually to the overthrow of capitalists and property owners and the triumph of the working classes.

* By the end of the Second World War economic history had emerged as a discipline in its own right. Economic historians continued to be interested in the process of industrialisation, but other issues, such as urbanisation and, in particular, economic growth, came into prominence. With the advent of the computer, some economic historians have become fascinated with methods of quantitative analysis. These techniques are used to study the mechanisms of economic growth, and to measure the extent of success or failure in business enterprise. In some ways this branch of the discipline has become more closely allied to pure economics than to history. Mainstream economic historians have progressed a long way from the purely descriptive writing of their pre-war predecessors. They have become increasingly specialised into areas of commercial, urban, agricultural and industrial history, using different techniques to analyse the process of economic change and continuity.

* Social history was not recognised as a separate discipline until the 1960s. It is no longer possible to think of social history as history with the politics left out because it has expanded into a major, if not *the* major, area of historical study. The earlier preoccupation with the life-style of the elites has been replaced by an interest in the whole structure of society and an analysis of social mobility and the processes of social change. Much of this new approach has been allied to the techniques of the social sciences, with an emphasis on industrialisation, urbanisation and the emergence of capitalism. Consequently, Marxist theories and the concept of class conflict have featured prominently in much of the recent work in this area. Social historians have been quick to adopt the techniques and ideas of anthropologists and psychologists, and this has led to an emphasis on the history of the family as a central social unit. At the same time it has been thought necessary to investigate the lives of people at all levels of society.

This has led to the development of an approach which has been called the history of 'mentality'. Although these techniques are closely related to the history of ideas, they aim to discover how groups of people and communities thought collectively. As a result there has been a considerable increase in research into popular culture and disorder. Another significant development is in the study of gender and women's history.

Possibly for the first time historians are approaching the goal of 'total' history sought by the *Annales* school earlier in the century. It has been suggested that social history is now about the totality of the life of people from every level of society. However, it must be remembered that all historians have their own interests and attitudes and are never entirely detached observers of the past. They select the sources and the evidence to make their own interpretation of history.

2 Sources of Evidence and Problems of Interpretation

A major difficulty with historical sources, particularly written ones, is that the further a historian goes back in time the harder such evidence is to find. The earlier past has been likened to a gigantic jigsaw puzzle with many of the essential pieces missing. This is both because older records are more likely to have been lost or destroyed, and for the reason that few people could read or write and therefore little was written down in the first place. Such difficulties create enormous problems for historians investigating the sixteenth century, particularly when they are trying to probe into the lives of the illiterate masses.

For Victorian historians and those of the early twentieth century whose main interest was in the lives of the elites this problem was not so great. This was a group with the political power and literacy to leave behind records which were likely to be preserved. Their role in government is recorded in state papers; the minutes of the privy council and parliament, and in other official records. The elites owned property and wealth the details of which may be preserved in wills, inventories, account books and estate surveys. In some cases their great houses, inhabited by their descendants, still exist. This type of evidence often reveals much about the lives of wives and children within the family circle. In addition, such sources as letters, diaries, portraits, furniture and toys can give a very full picture of this section of society. However, the lower the historian tries to probe down the social ranks, the scarcer becomes this type of evidence. Even those people who were not destitute tended to be less literate, and had fewer possessions to leave behind. Consequently they were less likely to write diaries or letters, or to draw up wills and inventories of their property. The homeless, without work or possessions, are likely to appear only in the records of the law courts, or in those of the overseers of the poor.

* A particular problem for the historian dealing with written sources of any type is how to interpret their evidence. A major difficulty (and this applies equally whether the source is written in English, French or Latin) is that the use and meaning of words in the sixteenth century was different from modern usage, and could vary in different parts of the country. Moreover, official records represent only the views of those in authority, while letters and diaries reflect the attitudes and beliefs of the writers. Politicians are unlikely to record their mistakes, or, at least, they will portray them in the best possible light. Equally, official accounts of popular rebellions and riots are unlikely to document accurately the views of the offenders. Court records give a very one-sided view of the lives of the people brought to justice. Historians of women's history complain that such evidence was written by men for men and, as such, gives a very poor representation of the lives and aspirations of women. Usually only elite women were sufficiently educated to leave written evidence. Most (normally estimated to be about 90 per cent) women could not read or write, and so they share the obscurity of the illiterate masses.

Similar problems apply to a variety of official documents utilised by the historian to measure such things as population levels, the standard of living, and levels of wealth and income. Taxation lists, muster certificates (recording men capable of military service), indices of wages and prices, and local censuses and surveys are primarily concerned with adult men with property, or in employment. This means that the homeless, the poor, the unemployed, women and children remain virtually invisible. Moreover, the uneven survival rate, possible inaccuracies, and regional variations of such sources make it difficult for historians to be sure that they are comparing like with like. Even such things as weights and measures and wage rates were different in virtually every county and town. Quantities of many commodities were calculated in volume by a measure such as a tun, the standard size of which varied in different parts of the country. Moreover, weights and measures differed between commodities, so that a tun of flour was 1800 pounds, but a tun of sugar or butter weighed 2240 pounds, while one of rice was only 1600 pounds. For the historian seeking a broad national picture of society even the parish registers, which were supposedly kept in standard form from 1538, present similar difficulties. Many have been lost, destroyed by fires, or eaten by rats. In any case the value of their information is very heavily dependent upon the care with which they were compiled. It is clear that the historian of the sixteenth century is faced with great difficulties in trying to recreate an accurate picture of life in the period.

* In an attempt to overcome these problems and to probe deeper into the 'invisible' sectors of society, historians have begun to adopt new approaches. The techniques of archaeology are being used to investigate deserted houses and village sites to find out more about the lives of the ordinary people. Evidence, such as fragments of pottery, animal bones, tools, ornaments and even the pollen from the soil, can reveal much about the lifestyle, diet and environment of the lower orders. Landscape history is being used to trace how social and economic developments altered the countryside and the way of life of those living in it. Attempts have been made to use the experience of anthropologists in studying modern illiterate societies to gain a greater insight into the motivations and loyalties of local communities. For the same purpose,

greater attention is being paid to folklore, popular ballads, dialect and local customs. However, it must be remembered that it is very difficult to recreate a full or accurate picture of sixteenth-century England. Any general study can, at best, only show how some of the people, in some places, lived at a particular moment. This cannot be called 'total' history. Only in very localised county and parish studies can historians, with a very good grasp of the sources and a wide range of techniques, hope to come close to achieving this end.

3 Issues, Theories and Approaches

Historians use this great range of scarce and often conflicting evidence to reach a variety of interpretations of the Tudor economy and society. Analysis of the changes leading towards industrialisation still remains a central feature of the approaches adopted by both social and economic historians. Social and economic change is seen as a very long-term process, stretching over centuries rather than decades. This means that the underlying continuity is considered to be just as important as the actual changes. In these terms the sixteenth century must be considered to be a very short time span. However, many historians think that certain features of the sixteenth century, such as the Renaissance, the Reformation, or the spread of capitalism or population growth, were particularly significant. This has led to the creation of some general theories, especially by Marxist, revisionist, and demographic historians, (see below) to explain the underlying processes taking place. While such theories form an important part of any discussion of the Tudor economy and society, it is now widely agreed that they are too vague to offer a full explanation. For this reason they are being constantly criticised and revised. Although this has caused a great deal of debate, led to the examination of fresh types of evidence, and created new interpretations, it has so far only confirmed the great complexity of historical change.

   * In broad terms, it is thought that a significant change in the process of modernisation dates from the middle of the fourteenth century. There is general agreement that this break in continuity, or 'watershed', was the so-called 'fourteenth-century crisis'. It is thought that this led to a number of crucial social, demographic, industrial and commercial changes that lasted until the middle of the sixteenth century. This phase is considered to have been ended by a short-term economic recession, which, in turn, introduced another period of development lasting to about 1650. Consequently, in England, the sixteenth century can be divided into two distinct parts as far as social and economic change is concerned. Of course there was considerable continuity and this has led a number of historians to talk in terms of the 'long sixteenth century', which ran from 1500 (or even 1450) to 1650. Although most historians concur with this general chronology, there is little agreement

about the causes, nature and significance of the events taking place. This is particularly true as regards the 'fourteenth-century crisis' itself.

* Orthodox Marxist historians, such as R. Brenner, who see historical change in terms of long-term social and economic processes, consider that the 'fourteenth-century crisis' was caused by a break-down in landlord-tenant relationships. The elites, the king, the Church, the nobles and the lesser landlords, relied on the taxes, rents and tithes collected from the peasantry for their income. In Marxist terms this is called 'surplus extraction'. By the fourteenth century it is thought that rising prices forced the elites to increase taxes, rents and tithes in order to support their expensive life-styles and military costs. This is considered to have represented 'over-surplus extraction', and to have led to great resentment among the peasantry. The result was rent strikes and increasing popular discontent, ending in the Peasants' Revolt of 1381. Although the rebellion was crushed, peasant resistance continued in the form of the abandonment of smallholdings. During the fifteenth century this forced the elites to replace labour services with cash rents, and to reduce rent levels drastically. This seriously undermined the economic position of the great landlords – the king, the Church and the nobles – whose incomes depended on rents from their estates. By the beginning of the sixteenth century the smaller landowners, or gentry, had taken advantage of the situation to use their smaller but more efficient estates for commercial farming. For this purpose they were able to recruit extra wage labour from among the families of the peasantry who had left their smallholdings. This approach sees the commercialisation of agriculture as the major explanation of social and economic change. The gentry are considered to be a new bourgeois class employing wage labour. It was this that changed relationships from landlord and peasant to employer and employee, and so marked a change in the 'mode of production' from feudal to capitalist.

* Demographic historians interpret changes in population levels to form a completely different explanation of the 'watershed'. They support J. Hatcher's view that there was a 'Malthusian crisis' (where rising levels of population outstrip the available food supplies) in the fourteenth century. It is suggested that by 1300 the population of England had risen to about six million. The steady demographic increase from the eleventh century had created a shortage of land, which forced both the clearance of woodland and the settlement of poorer marginal land. Over-cropping led to soil exhaustion and harvest failures by the beginning of the fourteenth century. In turn, this caused malnutrition and death from starvation in many parts of England. Population increase was checked and demographic levels fell, although they had begun to recover when the country was ravaged by bubonic plague – the Black Death of 1349. It is thought that about two million people died in the initial outbreak of the disease, and that this ended pressure on land and food supplies. Moreover, further plague epidemics, of varying intensity, reduced the population to as little as 1.5 million by the middle of the fifteenth century. This completely reversed the economic position. Food prices fell rapidly and there was a surplus of land and a shortage of labour. The great landowners, who relied on rents and the sale of foodstuffs from their estates, suffered a serious economic set-back. They were forced to reduce rents and to end labour services in order to attract tenants. Furthermore, they abandoned commercial farming and often had to lease out of their demesnes (land farmed directly by the owner and usually not rented out) at low rentals for long terms of up to 99 years. The gentry and more prosperous peasant farmers, or yeomen, were able to take advantage of the situation to increase the size of their estates and farms. They became the main commercial producers of foodstuffs and employers of wage labour. Although many peasant families took the opportunity to expand the size of their smallholdings, others left the land in order to benefit from the higher wage rates created by the shortage of labour. They provided the workforce for the commercial gentry and yeomen.

The Marxist and demographic interpretations of the 'fourteenth-century crisis' represent it in terms which involve the whole of society and explain the emergence of capitalism. Revisionist historians think that it was more a crisis within the feudal system, and involved only the landowning elites. They consider that it was a break-down in relationships between the Crown and the powerful feudal nobility. The cause was the dynastic problems and tensions created by the Hundred Years War against France in the fourteenth and fifteenth centuries. As a result, when the English were driven out of most of their French possessions by 1450, England collapsed into the civil conflict of the Wars of the Roses. By the end of the fifteenth century the Crown is seen as having succeeded in curbing both the political and economic power of the nobility. Revisionist historians, such as H. Trevor Roper, see a strong centralised state emerging under the Yorkists and early Tudor kings, upon whom the landed elites had to rely for their privileges and position. With the expansion of the government, office-holding increased, so giving the Crown great patronage and influence. This growth in bureaucracy is seen as benefiting the gentry, who began to take a greater role in both central and local government. While this interpretation emphasises the importance of the state and explains the rise of the gentry, it pays little attention to commercial forces, and ignores changes among the lower ranks of society.

* These three interpretations of the 'fourteenth-century crisis' are generally accepted, to a greater or lesser extent, by most historians as very useful starting-points from which to analyse economic and social change in the sixteenth century. Demographic historians stress that variations in population levels were the driving force behind social and economic change. They consider that rising levels of population, inflation, the standard of living and problems over food supplies are

central to any understanding of Tudor England. Marxist historians agree that the emergence of capitalism and the underlying class conflict are fundamental issues in sixteenth-century England.

However, they fail to reach any consensus over the basic causes of such developments. Orthodox Marxist analysis considers that the commercialisation of agriculture, which was forcing the peasantry off the land, was the central issue. This is seen as expanding the new employer/wage-earner relationship, considered to be breaking down the traditional village community solidarity. These changes are considered to be at the root of the popular discontent, or class conflict, characteristic of sixteenth-century England. Other Marxist historians, such as P. Kriedte and L. Medick, while not totally disagreeing with this interpretation, attach greater importance to the growth of industry. They consider that the development of the rural cloth industry from the thirteenth century was central to the spread of capitalism. This new system of cottage industry, which has been defined as proto-industrialisation, is seen as leading to the Industrial Revolution of the late eighteenth and nineteenth centuries. Some Marxist historians agree with I. Wallerstein that the rise of the state as an economic force, with the development of long-distance overseas trade and the establishment of colonies, was essential for the growth of capitalism. Revisionist historians agree that the rise of the state was highly significant. However, they see it in political and social terms, with the royal court and London becoming the centre of power and patronage, particularly under Elizabeth I.

* While historians outside these main schools of thought agree that such general theories are useful as tools of analysis, they consider that they give only a very partial view of Tudor England. A number of approaches drawing on the skills of other disciplines have been developed to gain greater insight into the complexity and regional variety of the changes taking place in the sixteenth century. Urban historians support P. Clark's emphasis on the importance of developments in towns, and in particular London, to explain the process of social and economic development occurring at all levels of society. Some historical geographers consider that a deterioration in the climate from the thirteenth century had a marked impact on agriculture and the problems of subsistence. Agricultural historians, while agreeing with J. Thirsk about the importance of agrarian change, are deeply divided over whether such developments were evolutionary or revolutionary. Many industrial historians are equally divided about the evolutionary or revolutionary nature of the historical process, and some are totally opposed to the theory of proto-industrialisation (see page 35). Moreover, they cannot agree whether developments in heavy industry, based on coal and iron, or those relying on agricultural products, such as textiles and leather, were the most significant. Historical anthropologists emphasise the importance of the family to any understanding of the

process of social development. At the same time there has been much analysis of the role of the family as an economic unit in the process of industrialisation.

* Recently an increasing number of historians have been paying considerable attention to discovering more about the lowest sections of society. This has led to the appearance of a number of studies about public order and popular disorder and rebellion. At the same time there has been some revision of views about the causes and treatment of poverty. Greater insights into the impact of social change have been gained by the study of popular culture. In this area there are two closely related issues. There is still debate about the extent to which the effects of the Renaissance, the Reformation and increased education were separating elite and popular culture anywhere in England except in Elizabethan London. Moreover, it is still unclear whether these same forces were having any real influence upon the traditional community life of the lower orders by 1600. Possibly the major growth area in historical research during the last few years has been in women's history at all levels of society, but particularly among the non-elites. Great attention has been given by R.A. Houlbrooke and M. Prior to the role of women and the family, and to the issue of whether commercialisation improved or worsened the position of women in society. Such approaches have helped historians to reach closer to the idea of 'total' history, but, as yet, they have not succeeded in producing a very clear picture of Tudor economy and society.

All these theories and issues will be examined in greater detail in the chapters which follow.

Making notes on 'Introduction: The Background'

This chapter is designed to introduce you to the variety of ways in which historians interpret the economic and social history of Tudor England. The first section shows how social and economic history has developed since the end of the nineteenth century. It is important that your notes should give you a clear chronological framework of these changes in approach so that you have a firm understanding of the thinking behind modern historical writing. You should study section two carefully to develop a sound grasp of the types of sources used by historians. Note down the various sources, how they are used, and the problems in interpreting them. Always remember that widely differing conclusions can be drawn from the same material by different historians. The last section examines three major general theories and some of the new approaches and interpretations being adopted by historians. Marxist, demographic and revisionist historians use different interpretations of the 'fourteenth-century crisis' to explain social, economic and political changes in Tudor England. It is important to have a clear grasp of these theories and interpretations because, although doubts have been cast on the accuracy of such general theories, they are still widely used by historians. At the same time take care to note the growing interest in lower order society, particularly in the history of women and the family.

CHAPTER 2

Population, Inflation and the Standard of Living

1 Introduction: Sources and their Interpretation

a) Population

There is general agreement among historians, based on the conclusions of E.A. Wrigley and R.S. Schofield, about the broad population trends prior to and during the sixteenth century. However, there is still much debate over the actual figures and the underlying causes of demographic change. The major difficulty is the nature of the sources which have to be used to calculate population levels in the early modern period, and the scarcity and uneven survival rate of such evidence. It was not until 1801 that a full national census was carried out. Although some local town and parish censuses have survived from the sixteenth century these are too isolated and infrequent to give any real indication of the population of England. The nearest that the historian can come to a national census for the sixteenth century is the muster certificates of 1522. These were drawn up for every parish and town to survey the number of men between the age of 16 and 60 available for military service. At the same time they were used to record wealth in the form of land holdings and moveable goods for a new tax assessment. The first problem with this evidence is that the returns have survived for only a limited number of counties, parishes and towns. Another difficulty is that, with the exception of gentlewomen and some female wage earners, only male heads of households and wage earners of military age are recorded. This means that women, children and the unemployed poor are rarely mentioned.

Similar difficulties apply to other national listings, such as the subsidy returns for taxation and other muster certificates later in the century, which demographers use to determine sixteenth-century population movements. In order to estimate the total population from the number of households given in these listings it is necessary to calculate the number of people likely to be living within the family group. This could include the husband and wife, children, a widowed parent and one or more servants, or it might be a single widower whose children had left home. However, most historians accept that by multiplying all the listed heads of household by 4.5, and than adding on between 10 and 30 per cent to account for the homeless poor not included in the listings, a reasonable estimate of population can be obtained. Partial support for this assumption comes from a local survey carried out in the Middlesex village of Ealing in 1599. There were 85 families of varying sizes living in the village, and the average number for a household was 4.75. Even so, not all historians agree that such calculations give a true estimate of total population levels, and there is much controversy over what percentage between 10 and 30 should be added to represent the homeless poor.

* Parish registers of births, marriages and deaths, which were increasingly being kept by all parishes after 1538, are very useful to supplement the meagre evidence of the national listings. Even allowing for the fact that many of them have been lost or destroyed, and the varying accuracy with which they were kept by the parish clergy, such registers contain a wealth of valuable evidence. One great advantage is that they list men, women and children from all sections of society, although it must be remembered that the homeless poor were less likely to come to church to be recorded. Because the dates of births, marriages and deaths are entered, it is possible to calculate life expectation and to construct family trees, sometimes over many generations. Such information can be followed up through the wills and inventories (lists of property) of members of the families when they are available. 'Family reconstruction' from such sources has been made much easier by the growing use of computing facilities, and has become one of the main ways in which historians examine demographic trends. This method, together with 'back projection' techniques whereby available data is used to make calculations for periods when the sources are inadequate, has enabled historians to reach much firmer conclusions about the general pattern of demography in the sixteenth century.

Parish registers are equally useful in many other respects. It is possible to determine the age of marriage of men and women. This is important for calculating fertility rates, because the number of children born generally depended on whether women were marrying earlier or later in life. If prices were high, land in short supply and employment opportunities low, the trend would be towards later marriage. It is also possible to determine the number and regularity with which children were born into families; this again is an indicator of economic conditions, because fewer children were likely to be born or survive in adverse conditions. Burial registers are very useful in calculating mortality rates in different age groups, sexes and times of the year. This type of information is essential in estimating demographic trends, and the impact of epidemics. Although cause of death was rarely recorded and Tudor medical knowledge was very inexact, it is possible to identify epidemics from the increased levels of mortality and from the time of the year when most deaths occurred. A sudden increase in deaths in the autumn is seen as indicating an influenza outbreak, while high mortality in the summer was more likely to be the result of bubonic plague. If the epidemic is seen to have killed mainly the old and infirm, then population recovery would probably have been rapid. However, if young women between the ages of 15 and 40 were the main victims, then recovery would most likely have been slow because this was the childbearing period.

b) Inflation and the Standard of Living

Sources of evidence about inflation and the standard of living are in many respects even more difficult to use. The main problem is that rents, prices, wages and measures varied widely all over the country. The price of grain in London is no indication of the effect of inflation on a craftsman living in York. Wage rates for building workers in the south of England tell the historian little about how well, or how badly, agricultural workers were faring in Wales. Moreover, this is only a small part of the difficulty. The central issue is whether an individual had access to land. Even in the larger towns all but the very poor had gardens and orchards, and in most cases rights of entry onto common land, which gave them some degree of self-sufficiency. In the country-side the great majority had their own gardens where they grew vegetables and kept chickens, and had a pig, and possibly a cow, which they were allowed to pasture on the village common. The consequence of this was that most people were, to a greater or lesser degree, independent of the full effect of market forces. This is why enclosure, which by fencing off common land and thus making it private, denied access to the lower orders and was a cause of widespread popular discontent in Tudor England. Similarly, because work was very seasonal, most people, including many of those living in towns, had more than one occupation. A Derbyshire miner might have a small-holding and with it access to common land where he could raise horses or cattle. A husbandman in the Fenlands might own a gun for wildfowling or share in the ownership of a boat as a part-time fisherman. The existence of this 'dual' economy makes it extremely difficult for the historian to draw any concrete conclusions about the standard of living enjoyed by any section of society. However, it is clear that the 400 per cent inflation between 1500 and 1600 had adversely effected a majority of the lower orders.

2 Interpretations of Demographic Change

Demographic historians maintain that the study of population change is central to any understanding of economic and social history. In particular, they suggest that, as alterations in population levels were the major cause of inflation or deflation, they determined whether there was economic growth or decline. Other historians do not attach such importance to demographic trends, but they do recognise their signi-ficance. All historians see population increase during the sixteenth century as a central issue in any consideration of social and economic change. It is thought that England may have been returning to a situation where the number of people were outstripping the available food supplies, and that the country was sliding into the 'Malthusian trap' of a subsistence crisis. There is considerable discussion as to the possibility of such a situation and, if so, whether it was national or merely localised. Shortages in expanding towns can be attributed to overcrowding and the inadequacies of the national road and river transport system. This can also explain local dearths resulting from over-specialisation in agriculture and grain hoarding by speculators. However, in general it is thought that adverse weather conditions (see page 41), not over-population, were the main cause of any apparent Malthusian crises.

Even so food prices were highly important to the lower orders, especially in towns. The purchase of foodstuffs, particularly grain, could absorb two-thirds of their income. For this reason the availability and price of grain is seen as a major determinant of the standard of living among the non-elites. Equally, population levels influenced living standards by determining the availability of land and the size of the labour force. Consequently, increasing population would force up the level of rents, force down wages and reduce opportunities for employment. All these inflationary tendencies are seen as major problems for successive Tudor governments, as they created poverty and popular discontent (see page 113).

* Apart from the central issue of rising or falling population, other demographic movements are seen as having a crucial effect on society and the economy. A growth in the amount of geographical mobility, as more people left the land to seek alternative employment, is regarded as a major feature in sixteenth-century England. The Tudor authorities called such movement 'vagrancy' and considered it to have a destabilising effect on the social structure. They blamed enclosure and the commercialisation of farming for the drift away from the land and considered this to be a cause of rural depopulation and popular discontent. While agreeing over the causes of such population movement, historians are divided about its consequences. Economic historians consider that rising population and enclosure were the basic causes of the growing geographical movement, and see such changes as economically beneficial. Enclosures and agricultural improvements are regarded as the major means by which food production was increased and the danger of subsistence crises averted. Moreover, they consider that the movement of people away from farming into more advanced forms of employment, such as industry, was a sign of economic progress. While agreeing about the causes of rural change, social historians see the consequences in a very different light. For them enclosure and commercialisation broke-up the traditional farming communities and created unemployment, poverty and destitution.

Closely related to these issues is the impact that the movement of people from the land had upon the towns. It is agreed that many of those leaving the villages, especially the young and unmarried of both sexes, drifted into towns, in particular London, to look for work. Many urban historians consider that this created additional problems. Town industries were craft based and had small, skilled workforces, and so were unable to employ the increasingly high numbers of semi-skilled and unskilled migrants. In addition, the influx of people is seen as putting an enormous strain on housing and food supplies in the towns. This 'urban crisis' is regarded as being a major reason for England's poor economic performance in the sixteenth century and a cause of social hardship and discontent. Other urban historians, who consider urbanisation as a major factor in economic growth, see the demographic expansion in the towns as beneficial. As towns were dependent on the surrounding countryside for food supplies, they see rising urban demand as central to the growth of market forces and the spread of commercialisation. This, they consider, was to lead, eventually, to economic growth, full employment and rising standards of living.

All these interpretations are very plausible, and it is often difficult for a student to choose between them. However, it must be said that, although some people at all social levels benefited from these changes, for the majority of the lower orders in England the sixteenth century was a time of considerable hardship. This was especially true during the closing decades, when the poverty and falling standards of living contrasted sharply with the comparative affluence of the lower orders at the opening of the century.

3 Demographic Change 1450–1550

Demographic historians regard the 'fourteenth-century crisis' as having been caused by sudden and drastic changes in the population level (see page 6). It is thought that, having fallen from a high point of around six million in 1300 to about 1.5 million (all national population figures are for England and Wales) by the middle of the fifteenth century, population then began to recover. The question which causes a great deal of debate is why the population began to increase again. A straightforward answer is that the enormous demographic drop had created a 'Malthusian paradise' in the fifteenth century. With such a low density of people there was an ample supply of land, so that there were plenty of vacant smallholdings available at low rents. At the same time, lack of demand kept food prices low, and shortages of labour pushed wage levels up. This meant that young people were able to marry earlier. In normal conditions the English inheritance custom of primogeniture meant that the eldest son who inherited the family smallholding had to wait until his father died before he could get married. Younger sons and daughters generally left home to work as apprentices or servants in husbandry or industry until their mid-twenties to save enough to be able to afford to get married. However, in the fifteenth century, cheap food and high wages enabled many to get married earlier. This meant that wives had a longer period of fertility and consequently had more children, so that by the end of the century the population had begun to rise.

   * Although this explanation is very convincing, many demographers consider that mortality rates, not fertility rates, are the major determinants of population levels in pre-industrial societies. They question why, if fertility was the principal element, it took a hundred years for demographic recovery to begin. It is agreed that the sudden drop in population in the fourteenth century resulted from high death rates caused by the Black Death of 1349 and the ensuing plague cycle. Hence it is claimed that the subsequent recovery must have been brought about by a change in mortality rates, and not simply because of earlier marriage. The difficulty with this argument is that there is no obvious reason why the death rate should have declined. Bubonic plague was still endemic in England, together with a number of equally virulent diseases, such as influenza, cholera, typhus and malaria. However, it is suggested that by the late fifteenth century the population had begun to build-up an immunity to the bubonic plague. In addition some historians suggest that, whereas initially the plague had attacked all age groups indiscriminantly, it gradually became more selective. The old and infirm became the most vulnerable, whereas young adults, and particularly young women, had greater immunity. This, it is claimed, would mean that more children were likely to be born, so leading to population increase. An alternative suggestion is that infants and young children became less vulnerable, and this again would lead to eventual demographic recovery. These forces acting together are thought to have lowered the age profile and produced a high proportion of young people in England by the end of the century.

   * Whatever explanation is accepted, it is considered that by the 1520s the population had reached about 2.3 million. This calculation is based on the muster certificates of 1522 and subsidy returns for 1524 and 1525 (see page 11). On this evidence the population was still 62 per cent below the level in 1300. However, such estimates are very imprecise, and local studies reveal considerable variations all over the country. The village of Stanford in the Vale in Berkshire is a good example of such differences in demographic rates of recovery. In 1307 a manorial survey shows that the village had 78 households, which gives an estimated population of 456. The muster certificate for 1522 shows that the number of households had fallen to 47, suggesting that the population was 274, only 40 per cent below the figure for 1307. Such a discrepancy might indicate that by 1307 Stanford in the Vale had suffered from the early fourteenth-century famines (see page 6), and that its population had already fallen from the medieval peak. Equally,

it might be that the village had experienced lower than average mortality rates, or that its rate of recovery was greater than elsewhere. Similar variations were common all over the country. There were considerable differences in mortality and recovery rates between town and countryside, as well as between individual towns and even neighbouring villages. This makes it very difficult to obtain a precise picture of the level of demographic increase by the 1520s. Certainly, contemporary writers were not particularly aware of any significant rise in population level. They still thought that the country was badly under-populated, and wrote gloomily of the empty houses and vacant plots of land in towns and villages.

  * This phase of population expansion is thought to have continued until the middle of the century, by which time the government was beginning to talk about over-population. It is estimated that there was a demographic growth of one per cent a year, and that by 1550 the population had reached just over three million. However, the rate of growth was uneven, and this, alongside the local variations makes it very difficult to identify any underlying trend. The additional evidence supplied by the parish registers after 1538 suggests that the main phase of growth came in the 1540s. Historians are divided as to how to explain this pattern. If earlier marriage and greater fertility were the reasons for population recovery, it is difficult to see why the rate of growth was so slow up to 1540. Even by 1550, when the population had reached three million, it was still only half what it had been in 1300. For most of the first half of the sixteenth century there was no undue pressure on the land. This suggests that the conditions should have been almost as favourable as they had been in the fifteenth century. Rents were still relatively low, wages comparatively high and there was no shortage of job opportunities.

  It has been suggested that the sluggish rate of demographic growth might have been the result of a deterioration in the climate. A long period of settled and comparatively warm weather is thought to have ended during the thirteenth century. The change was marked by a fall of some two degrees centigrade in average temperatures, and an increase in rainfall. These new conditions are considered to have shortened the growing season, and to have made many areas unsuitable for cereal growing. However, the 'Mini Ice Age' is not thought to have ended until the eighteenth century, during which time the demographic trend was consistently upward. This makes it difficult to say more than that in the long term the rate of recovery might have been quicker had it not been for the poorer climatic conditions. In the short term, the more unsettled weather may well have caused more frequent runs of bad harvests, such as those of 1527–9, which acted as temporary checks to population growth.

  * Most historians still favour the view that mortality rates, resulting from endemic disease, were the main reason for the slow demographic

growth up to 1540, and also explain the population explosion in the 1540s. It is thought that at the end of the fifteenth century a new killer virus, the 'English sweat', became endemic. This disease took the form of a fever, which spread more rapidly than bubonic plague and could kill within 24 hours. It was particularly virulent between 1485 and 1528 and, because young adults were the most vulnerable to the disease, it is thought that this is the main reason for the slow population growth up to 1540. At the same time there were four serious plague outbreaks between 1500 and 1528, and another in the late 1530s, with, in the latter case, young adolescents being the most vulnerable group. Apart from this one visitation of plague, England appears to have suffered no serious epidemics between 1528 and 1550 and this, it is thought, might well account for the sudden increase in population in the 1540s. Furthermore, it is suggested that there was a drop in infant mortality, which meant that more children survived into adulthood. In addition, there was a run of good harvests from 1537 to 1542, and from 1546 to 1548. It is considered that these favourable harvests, coinciding with the absence of epidemics, accentuated the underlying demographic trend.

Although population is thought to have peaked in 1550, there are some suggestions that there might have been a potential Malthusian subsistence crisis by 1549. The run of good harvests was followed by a very poor harvest is 1549. Sir Thomas Smith, Secretary to the Privy Council, writing in the same year, certainly thought that it was bad enough to be called a 'dearth' or famine year. There were popular rebellions in Norfolk and the West Country, and serious riots in the Midlands and southern England. The main focus of popular discontent was the government's failure to stop the enclosure of arable and common land (see page 20), which was blamed for the high price of grain. Popular unrest is thought to have been heightened because of the previous run of good harvests, which had brought down the price of grain and so raised living standards and increased expectations among the lower orders. Paradoxically, this run of good harvests possibly made the situation worse by 1549. Commercial farmers, faced by falling profits, are thought to have switched to more lucrative sheep and cattle production, so reducing grain supplies. At the same time, greater regional agricultural specialisation may well have created local shortages, which were aggravated by the poor transport system. However, most historians doubt that there was a genuine subsistence crisis in 1549. They feel that the widespread discontent was heightened by the unpopularity of the government, high inflation and opposition to the introduction of religious reforms.

The population picture up to 1550 is far from clear, and it is further complicated by the local variations. Demographic recovery depended very much upon the two variables: population density and incidence of disease. Towns, in particular London, had greater concentrations of population than the surrounding countryside. For this reason they were susceptible to epidemics, and had high mortality rates. At the same time, towns had a high birthrate and were attractive to migrants from the countryside, which meant that their recovery rate was high. However, because of the random nature of epidemics there were considerable differences in fortune between individual towns. A survey of the Berkshire market town of Wantage in the 1550s estimated the town's population to be 1000, a figure which has been confirmed by calculations from the parish registers. The estimated population of Wantage in 1522 was 600; a demographic increase of 66 per cent in 30 years which was twice the national average. Other towns made much smaller gains and some even shrank in size. Norwich, Bristol and York, the three largest towns after London, all had severe epidemics during this period, and it is suggested that the population of Norwich remained static between 1522 and 1558. However, London, although it suffered epidemics, continued to expand and by the 1550s was facing severe unemployment problems. The town authorities blamed them on early marriage among young apprentices, who, it was claimed, set themselves up in a craft without having saved enough money to support a family. To prevent this it was ordered that no one should start a business before reaching the age of 24.

To a lesser degree there were considerable differences in densities of rural population. In broad terms the lowland south-east of England was more heavily settled than the upland north and west. Settlement was much greater in areas of arable farming than in forest and pastoral regions. However, the drift of smallholders from the land meant this pattern was constantly changing, especially by the end of the sixteenth century. A village that had undergone extensive enclosure might lose population through migration in contrast to a neighbouring village that remained unenclosed. Another consequence of increasing geographical mobility was that epidemics were spread more widely and with greater rapidity. Outbreaks depended upon the movements of the carriers of the disease. This meant that local epidemics could be random and isolated, so that one village might remained unscathed, while its neighbour was decimated. Under these circumstances it must be remembered that the demographic history of every town and village is different.

4 Demographic Change 1550–1600

The demographic pattern during the second half of the sixteenth century is more readily identifiable than it is for the first 50 years. It is clear that the authorities were becoming conscious that the population was increasing. While the governments earlier in the century had been worried about depopulation and a shortage of men of military age, under Elizabeth I the major concerns were vagrancy, unemployment and poverty. It is thought that by 1600 the population had reached just over four million; an increase of 25 per cent since 1550. This represents a slowing down in the rate of growth in comparison with the first half of the century. Even so, some historians consider that the population might have begun to outstrip food supplies by the end of the century, and there is some debate over whether there was a Malthusian subsistence crisis in the 1590s.

* Serious epidemics in the 1550s eased any population pressure that there might have been by 1549 and slowed down the rate of increase. There were renewed outbreaks of sweating sickness and plague in 1551 and 1552. Then the whole country was ravaged by devastating influenza epidemics between 1556 and 1558. The mortality rate of these latter outbreaks alone have been estimated to have been at least 6 per cent and, as a result, it is thought that the population may well have fallen below three million once again. To make matters worse, the harvests during the 1550s were well below average. Those between 1549 and 1551 were bad, and there was another series of failures in 1554, 1555 and 1556. The harvests of 1555 and 1556 were particularly bad and probably caused widespread famines and severe grain shortages in the towns. In 1550 fears over grain shortages and the possibility of popular rioting resulted in the passing of anti-enclosure legislation, which was designed to encourage husbandmen to return to the land and so increase grain output. In the event there was no widespread popular discontent, possibly because of the easing of population pressure. By 1561 the population is estimated to have fallen to 2,985,000.

* Elizabeth I was fortunate in that, in addition to the initial levelling off in demographic growth, there were no bad harvests during her reign until the late 1580s. Moreover, in 1566-71, 1582-4 and 1591-3 England enjoyed runs of exceptionally good harvests. Furthermore, after the famines of the mid-1590s, another run of good harvests began in 1601 which lasted until 1606. At the same time the country was remarkably free from serious epidemics. The sweating sickness virus seems to have disappeared after the 1550s, and outbreaks of plague and other diseases were confined mainly to the larger towns. These good conditions, it is considered, resulted in an increase in births over deaths. At the same time the fall in food prices is thought to have encouraged earlier marriage, and so brought improved fertility. After 1560 the population rose steadily every decade until the end of the century, by which time it had reached an estimated level of 4,110,000. The levelling off in grain prices until the late 1580s suggests that English agriculture, with the help of the settled weather, was able to feed a steadily rising population. However, it must be remembered that the estimated population in 1600 was still a third smaller than it had been 300 years previously. On the other hand, because of the drastic fall in late medieval population and the deterioration in the climate, large areas of land had gone out of cultivation since 1300. Whole regions, such as the Brecklands in

Norfolk, had been virtually abandoned, and all over the country former arable fields had been converted to pasture. At the same time, there had been a decrease in general farming with the development of specialist agriculture (see page 38).

In addition to the increase in homeless vagrants seeking work, there was a marked rise in the number of migrants moving into the towns during the second half of the century. It is estimated that urban dwellers rose from 5 per cent of the total population in the 1520s to approaching 10 per cent by 1600. In London alone the number of people grew from 50,000 to 200,000 over the same period, to represent half the urban population of the country, most of the increase occurring after 1570. Apart from Southampton, most other large towns showed a similar rapid growth in the second half of the century. This expansion took place even although there were serious outbreaks of plague, especially in Bristol and Norwich. In 1563 one outbreak is estimated to have caused 20,000 deaths in London alone. Such growth, in spite of high mortality rates from disease, is considered to indicate that the increase in urban population resulted from the volume of migration from the countryside. As towns were largely dependent on the surrounding countryside for food supplies, this represents a considerable increase in market demand on agricultural production.

Clearly demographic and other pressures were having an impact on the structure of rural society by 1600. The amount of change within a particular village was very variable, depending on location, whether it was arable or pastoral and if it had been enclosed. A good example of the nature of these changes on an unenclosed, arable settlement is the village of Hinton Waldrist in Berkshire. In 1522 there were 23 households, which gives an estimated population of 134. In 1587 a manorial survey records 34 households, suggesting that the population had risen to 199. This represents an increase of 43 per cent. Over the same period the national population is estimated to have risen from 2.3 to 3.8 million, an increase of 40 per cent. In demographic terms Hinton appears to have been fairly typical, but the figures do not reveal the structural change that had taken place in the village. In 1522 the 23 households consisted of three yeomen with about 60 acres of land each, eight self-sufficient husbandmen each with 30 acres, ten partly self-sufficient husbandmen with about 15 acres each and two cottagers each with only a garden and a few acres of land. By 1587 the picture was very different. There was one very prosperous yeoman farming 200 acres and holding seven of the village houses, six other yeomen each farming about 90 acres of land, and seven husbandmen each with 15 to 40 acres of land. In addition there were 14 cottagers, some with three acres of land and others with only their gardens. Clearly such changes had considerable implications for the living standards of the villagers (see page 29).

* The long spell of good harvests ended in the late 1580s and grain

prices began to rise. Then from 1594 there was a run of bad harvests lasting until 1597. The harvests in 1596 and 1597 were particularly bad, with wheat prices rising above the average by 82 per cent and 64 per cent respectively. By 1596 wheat prices stood at 50 shillings a quarter, twice what they had been in the early 1580s. This means that 1596 and 1597 were considered to be 'dearth' (famine) years, although part of the problem was that they followed two other bad seasons. Certainly there were shortages of grain, especially in London and the larger towns, although the improved efficiency of the urban authorities (see page 114) prevented any actual starvation. There were examples of chronic food shortages in the countryside, but these are considered to be isolated incidents, and it is not thought that there is any evidence of widespread famine. The problems of the mid-1590s have prompted speculation as to whether England was experiencing a subsistence crisis brought on by over-population. This idea has now been largely rejected. It is thought that the harvest failures were caused by bad weather. There is no evidence that over-production was causing soil exhaustion and crop failures. Local problems are considered to have been caused by regional specialisation and continued transport difficulties (see page 71). These views are supported by the renewed run of good harvests after 1601 and by the fact that there was no real check in the upward demographic movement. Most historians consider that by 1600 England had escaped from the 'Malthusian trap' of subsistence crisis which still plagued her continental neighbours.

5 Inflation 1450–1550

It has been estimated that inflation in England amounted to 400 per cent over the whole of the sixteenth century. Previously it was thought that the large quantities of gold and silver imported into Western Europe by Spain from South America was a major cause of English inflation. It is now considered that the influence of imported bullion was not really felt in England until the end of the century. Most historians agree with R.B. Outhwaite that rising population, which created greater demand, was the underlying cause of price rises. Of course the situation was much more complicated than just a simple matter of supply and demand, and it is not always possible to offer convincing explanations of the movement of prices in specific cases. However, other factors which influenced the situation can be identified. For example, spells of bad weather sometimes forced up prices, which were often slow in returning to their former level. Wars cut off the flow of imports and exports and created shortages and unemployment. At the same time the high cost of wars could affect taxation levels and so influence spending power. Wages and rent levels were important because they could increase production costs and so raise prices. Some historians stress the importance of the volume of money in circulation.

For them the confiscation of church gold and silver by Henry VIII and its conversion into coinage and the frequent debasements of the coinage were a major cause of inflation until the 1550s.

  * The drastic decline in population between 1350 and 1450 is seen as having been deflationary. Prices, rents and the value of land fell, and town populations shrank. Industrial output declined as demand was reduced, and because production costs rose as a result of the higher wage levels demanded by the reduced workforce. There was a general recession across Western Europe which lasted until the end of the fifteenth century. From about 1470, when it is thought that population began to recover, there was a slow reversal of the situation. As demographic levels increased prices began to rise in response to demand. The 'price scissors', the time at which prices and rents overtook wages, is considered to have occurred shortly after 1500. A sharp upward spiral continued until the 1550s. However, this inflationary pattern clearly cannot be explained entirely by upward demographic pressure.

Population levels rose only relatively slowly until 1540. Over the same period prices and rents increased at a much faster rate. In the towns the cost of grain and meat doubled between 1510 and 1530. The poor harvests during the 1520s are seen as contributing to this trend. However, this does not explain why grain prices did not fall after the run of good harvests in the 1530s, and why meat prices kept rising. Some historians see the upward movement of cereal prices as a consequence of commercial farming and enclosure. They consider that those farmers who had spent money on enclosure and land improvement expected a good return on their investment. As wool prices were higher than those for grain, because of the strong demand for English cloth and wool on the continent, it is thought farmers were more likely to use their land for sheep pasture than for the growing of cereals and the raising of animals for slaughter. Another possible explanation for the steady upward movement of both grain and meat prices is increased demand from the towns. Not only were urban population levels beginning to recover, particularly in London, but town dwellers were expecting a higher standard of living. It was this that increased the demand for meat.

The movements of wages and rents are equally inconclusive, and certainly do not indicate population pressure by 1540. In the south-east of England average rents are thought to have doubled from 6d to 13d an acre by the end of the 1530s. Increases were particularly noticeable near to towns, especially London, where the market for foodstuffs was buoyant. Rents for pasture were rising because of the high price of wool and the value of animal products. Improved and enclosed land was in demand, and it is thought that this also pushed up the rents on neighbouring land. However, away from the south-east rents were stationary, and may have been falling in some areas. Wage levels, which had risen to 4d a day for agricultural workers and 6d a day for building workers by about 1450, remained static for a century. This has prompted the suggestion that there was no great build-up of surplus labour by 1550 to tempt employers to try to force down wage levels, and that inflationary pressures do not appear to have been sufficient to prompt demands for higher wages.

    * During the 1540s there is evidence that pressure from inflation and higher population were both being felt in England. The runs of good harvests from the late 1530s to 1548 meant that grain prices stabilised, and so lowered the cost of living for most people. This, it is thought, encouraged earlier marriage and so caused a demographic increase of over one per cent a year in the decade up to 1550. The bad harvests of 1549 to 1551 once again raised the price of grain to about 28 shillings a quarter; three and a half times what it been in the 1520s. Sir Thomas Smith considered that by 1549 all prices for goods and services had at least doubled during his lifetime. He cites, as examples, that his shoes, which he used to buy for 6d, cost 1 shilling; a cap had risen in price from 1s 2d to 2s 5d; and the cost of shoeing a horse was 1 shilling instead of 6d. He blamed the 'dearth' in 1549 on the bad harvest and the commercial farmers and husbandmen who had converted arable land to pasture in order to profit from the high price of wool and other animal products. However, he attributed the overall inflation to debasement and the falling value of the English coinage.

    Historians generally agree with this viewpoint on the grounds that a rise in population from 2.3 to 3 million was insufficient in itself to explain inflation of 200 per cent over the first half of the century. Henry VIII first debased the coinage in 1526, by melting down the silver coins and reminting them with some of the silver replaced by copper, to help to finance his wars against France. He used this device again in 1543 when he was at war with France and Scotland. The continued need to raise money for military expenditure forced his successor, Edward VI, to make two further debasements of the coinage in 1548 and 1551. By then the silver content of the coins had been reduced to a quarter of the level in 1525. It is considered that by increasing the number of coins in circulation, while at the same time lowering their intrinsic value, the government was creating a very rapid inflation of prices. The situation was made still worse by the English Reformation which led the government to seize the gold and silver ornaments from monasteries and churches as they were regarded as objects of Catholic superstition. Most of these were melted down and turned into coins, so adding to the amount of debased coinage in circulation. Debasement, it is felt, accounts for the very high level of prices by 1550, and for the especially rapid rate of inflation in the 1540s.

6 Inflation 1550–1600

The dual effect of population increase and debasement can be seen to be working in reverse during the 1550s. Severe epidemics of plague, sweating sickness and influenza checked the rate of demographic increase, and by 1561 had reduced the population to below three million. At the same time the government had made peace with France and Scotland in 1550, and had begun to try to restore stability to the currency. In 1552 all the debased coins were collected in and reminted with the silver content restored to the level in 1527. This, together with the reduction in population, is thought to have slowed the rate of inflation. However, the poor harvests of the 1550s raised grain prices, and by 1556 they were five and a half times the level of the 1520s. In addition the collapse of the Antwerp cloth market in the 1550s (see page 46) caused widespread unemployment among textile workers in East Anglia and the West Country.

It is thought that prices at least doubled between 1540 and 1560. The price of sugar, for example, rose from 4d to 10d a pound, while the wholesale cost of a bale of cloth more than trebled from £2 to £7. At the same time the increased demand for houses and plots of land caused a marked rise in rents all over the country. In some places they rose from 13d to 20d an acre. Moreover it is thought that demand for freehold land was not influenced by the temporary drop in population because there were plenty of landless younger sons eager to marry and set up house. For the first time in the century there was some upward movement in wages. At the height of the influenza outbreak wages for harvest workers in some places rose to 12d a day, but this only indicated temporary shortages of labour and wages fell back as the effect of the epidemic diminished. In many parts of the country there were too few job vacancies to meet demand, a situation made worse by widespread unemployment following the slump in cloth exports. By 1560 agricultural wages had risen from 4d to 6d a day, while building and industrial wages were generally more than double this amount. However, when inflation is taken into account, agricultural wages were only 3.5d a day in real terms. This meant that the income of even industrial workers was scarcely keeping up with rising prices.

* The run of good harvests from the 1560s into the 1580s meant that population levels recovered quickly. Earlier marriages, because of the good food supply, and the relative absence of epidemics, led to a consistent population increase of some 6 per cent a year until the late 1580s. This restored the inflationary pressure of population growth and caused a continued upward spiral of prices. However, most historians consider that after 1560 population was rising faster than inflation, in contrast to the earlier part of the century when prices were increasing more rapidly than population. Consequently, although inflation over the whole century is estimated at 400 per cent, the greater part of this

increase is thought to have occurred by 1560. Of course this did not mean that price and rent levels did not continue to rise, so that the impact of inflation on the lower orders continued until 1600. In addition, it is thought that the importation of South American bullion into Western Europe was beginning to have some inflationary influence in England by increasing the amount of coinage in circulation. However, as the rate of inflation is now seen to have been slowing, the impact cannot have been as great as it was previously thought, and it certainly did not create the hyper-inflation caused by debasement in the 1540s.

Although the succession of good harvests until the late 1580s caused grain prices to fall and to level out at about 25 shillings a quarter, this did little to help the living standards of the lower orders. Demographic growth and the rise in urban population meant that grain prices were still three times above those of the 1520s At the same time population growth was increasing the pressure on the land and consistently forcing up rents. By 1600 the average rental had risen to 5 shillings an acre, ten times what it had been in 1500. Lower order living standards were further eroded because more people were becoming dependent on wages. As population rose the pool of surplus labour rose. In any case, the English textile industry was slow to recover from the slump in the 1550s, and industrial expansion was generally sluggish (see page 52). This meant that wage rates rose more slowly than prices.

* The situation was made worse by a return of poor harvests in the late 1580s and the succession of bad harvests in the mid-1590s. Even by 1590 the average price of wheat had risen to 35 shillings a quarter, and by 1596 stood at 50 shillings a quarter. It is clear that the government and the local authorities were well aware of the dangers of the situation:

Report of the Justices to the [Privy] Council concerning scarcity in Norfolk, 11 July 1586

 1 That for a further proceeding in the accomplishment of your honourable letters concerning the furnishing of the markets with corn, we have according to our former letters of the 9th of June last, met here together this day for conference therein. And
 5 perusing all our notes and proceedings together, we find that throughout this Shire by such order as we have taken with owners and farmers and also badgers [dealers] and buyers of corn and grain, the markets are by them plentifully served every market day with corn and the same sold at reasonable rates, viz wheat at
10 22 shillings the quarter, rye at 15 shilling, malt at 14 shillings and barley at 12 shillings, of which kinds of corn the poorer sort are by persuasion served at meaner [cheaper] prices.

An Act for the Maintenance of Husbandry and Tillage, 1597/8
 1 Be it enacted . . . that whereas any lands or grounds at any time

since the 17th of November in the first year of Her Majesty's
reign [1558] have been converted to sheep pastures or to the
fattening or grazing of cattle, the same lands having been tillable
5 [arable] lands, fields or grounds such as have been used in tillage
by the space of twelve years together at the least next before such
conversion, according to the nature of the soil and course [type] of
husbandry used in that part of the country, all such lands and
grounds as aforesaid shall, before the first day of May which shall
10 be in the year of Our Lord God 1599, be restored to tillage, or laid
for tillage in such sort as the whole ground, according to the
nature of the soil and course of husbandry used in that part of the
country, be within three years at the least turned to tillage by the
occupiers and possessors thereof, and so shall be continued
15 forever.

Such measures by the authorities did little to ameliorate conditions.
Although the price of grain fell back as harvests improved after 1597
wheat was still 30 shillings a quarter at the end of the century. The
effect of the rise in grain prices from the late 1580s was to cause many
couples to delay marriage. Later marriages appear to have significantly
reduced the birth-rate, and it is estimated that the rate of population
increase had dropped from 6 to 2.5 per cent by 1600. It is clear that
inflation trends in the sixteenth century confirm the underlying importance of demographic growth or decline on price, wage and rent levels.
At the same time, it is evident that the money supply and manipulations
of the currency, such as debasements, could have a rapid, short-term
influence. However, it is equally certain that the price of grain,
determined principally by weather conditions, was highly influential.
Not only could it have a very rapid short-term impact on the cost of
living for the majority of people, but it had long-term consequences on
the demographic trends. Variations in grain prices affected the age at
which many people married and therefore had an important influence
on population movements.

7 The Standard of Living

The research of R.H. Tawney, and more recently K. Wrightson, has
shown that it is difficult to assess the effects of inflation and population
increase by the end of the century in anything but general terms.
Broadly speaking, it is possible to say that those sections of society
which had suffered from the deflation of the fifteenth century gained
from the inflation of the sixteenth century, while the reverse is true for
those that had benefited from the deflationary conditions. This means
that the landed elites, yeomen, prosperous husbandmen, merchants
and self-employed craftsmen and industrialists generally improved
their economic position, while the lower orders became more impover-

ished. On the other hand, the variations in individual family fortunes, and of members within a family, meant that by no means everyone in either group were winners or losers. It is agreed that during the century the gap between rich and poor widened significantly and that this polarisation was just as marked in the countryside as in the towns. By 1600 it is considered that possibly 60 per cent of the population were living on or below the poverty line (see page 109).

    * By the end of the century it is possible to say that the aristocracy had benefited most from the inflationary conditions. As major landowners they gained not only from the sharp rise in rents, once the long-term leases granted in the fifteenth century had expired, but also from the high profits to be made from commercial farming and other enterprises. The gentry, yeomen and prosperous husbandmen benefited similarly, but to a lesser degree, because they frequently leased land and so suffered from rising rents. Merchants, craftsmen, industrialists and other employers were helped by high price levels and the falling value of employees' wages. On the other hand, market demand was sluggish, the cost of raw materials steadily increased and overseas trade fluctuated, which meant that any business enterprise carried a considerable degree of risk. Among all these groups, families were just as likely to fail and fall into destitution as they were to create large fortunes. Many people thought of life as a wheel of fortune which carried some to the top and many to the bottom.

    * There was a similar diversity of fortune among the lower orders, although it is true to say that for them failure was much more likely than was success. The constant upward spiral of prices and rents, falling real wages and the shortage of land eroded the standard of living for the great majority. Even the self-employed small craftsmen and the semi-self-sufficient husbandmen in the countryside were just as likely to be adversely affected as the wage earners. Illness, a slump in trade or a bad harvest could easily plunge them into poverty. However, it is very difficult for the historian to judge the full impact of inflation because most of the lower orders, whether in town or country, had more than one occupation during the year. Equally, the amount of independence from the market, and the degree of self-sufficiency even in the humblest of families, makes it virtually impossible to gauge the impact of rising prices in general terms. Here access to land, whether a garden or common land, was all important. Clearly, as the privatisation of land progressed during the sixteenth century, and urban populations increased, a greater percentage of the lower orders found it difficult to remain immune from market forces. However, apprentices and living-in servants in agriculture and industry were provided with food and clothes, while many wage labourers were given meals or gifts of foodstuffs to take home. Furthermore, the widespread use of barter in the exchange of goods and payments in kind rather than actual money

meant that changes in the value of the currency often had little effect on the lower orders.

The anxieties of the London authorities in the 1550s over the plight of young craftsmen (see page 19) is a good instance of the impact of inflation in the towns. The village of Hinton Waldrist in Berkshire (see page 21) provides an equally valuable insight into living conditions in the countryside. In 1522, apart from the three yeomen and two cottagers, the villagers were small farmers of roughly equal wealth and status. By 1587 only seven of the original families still lived in the village and most of the land was farmed by eight families. The remainder of the villagers were cottagers who worked on the land of their richer neighbours. As the village was still largely unenclosed, the cottagers had access to the common land and so retained some degree of self-sufficiency. However, it is clear that changes in the standard of living had not just widened the wealth gap between rich and poor, but had created social stratification among the lower orders. It is thought that cottagers living in enclosed arable parishes without access to common land were likely to be more adversely influenced by rising prices than those living in unenclosed villages. Equally it can be said that those migrants who were moving in increasing numbers into the unenclosed woodland and pasture parishes could retain more independence than their counterparts in arable areas.

* In overall terms historians consider that inflation had the greatest impact on the living standards of the old and the young among the lower orders. Ageing parents whose children had left home and widows and widowers appear to have been one group particularly badly hit by rising food prices. They are thought to have suffered during dearth years and to have been particularly vulnerable to the epidemics at the end of the century. The increasing shortage of land to rent and rising levels of unemployment forced many younger sons and daughters to leave their native villages and towns to find work and somewhere to live. Some historians consider that young women working in agriculture were especially badly affected because of the growing surplus of labour. It is thought that they were increasingly forced out of better paid work, such as harvesting, which became male occupations, into low status tasks such as weeding and bird scaring. This added to the difficulties of young couples trying to save enough to be able to marry. Although worsening economic conditions did not stop early marriage in periods of low grain prices, it is thought that the sequence of bad harvests was sufficient to cause a general rise in the age of marriage among the lower orders by the late 1580s. By the end of the century most of the vagrants seeking work seem to have been young, single men and women between the ages of 15 and 25. Certainly for them England was no longer the 'Malthusian paradise' that it had been at the beginning of the century.

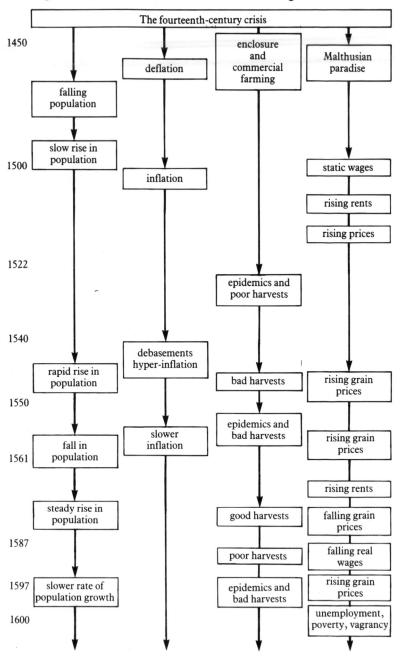

Summary – Population, Inflation and the Standard of Living

Making notes on 'Population, Inflation and the Standard of Living'

Population increase and inflation are regarded as key issues in any study of sixteenth-century English economy and society. Demographic historians see such movements as a major determinant of social and economic change. However, it is important to remember that some writers, particularly Marxist historians, consider other factors to be just as, if not more, important. Moreover, because the sources of evidence are so difficult to interpret, there is considerable debate and controversy among historians about the significance of the changes taking place. The first section outlines some of the major sources used by historians to measure these type of changes. It is important for you to note how they are used and the problems associated with them. The second section examines various interpretations of demographic change. You should note the ways in which historians measure population movements and the effects of inflation and how their interpretations differ. Sections three and four compare the demographic trends in the first and second halves of the century. Make sure that you have a clear grasp of the chronology of the demographic trend between 1450 and 1600 and of the explanations given for the changes. Take care to note other factors, such as migration, which caused local variations. The next two sections make a similar comparison of the inflationary trends. It is equally important that you have a clear picture of the pattern of inflation over the same period. Note all the possible causes of inflation, such as harvest failures and debasement of coinage, apart from the underlying population increase. The final section explores changes in the standard of living across all social ranks. Deflation followed by demographic increase and inflation had a considerable impact on living standards between 1450 and 1600. Be careful to note how and why the fortunes of all sections of society changed over the period. However, remember that there were great variations between individuals and within all social groups.

Answering essay questions on 'Population, Inflation and the Standard of Living'

Examiners regularly set questions on the causes and effects of the rise of population and inflation in sixteenth-century England. Thus there are four obvious issues on which to concentrate – i) the causes of the rise in population, ii) the effects of the rise in population, iii) the causes of inflation and iv) the effects of inflation. All the following questions have to do with one or more of these issues:

1. Discuss the view that 'the main cause of economic and social change in Tudor England was the rise in population'.
2. Who gained and who lost from the price rise in Tudor England?
3. For what reasons did some of the peasantry and some of the gentry in England become richer during the sixteenth century, while at the same time some members of these groups became poorer?
4. What were the causes and consequences of inflation in Tudor England?
5. 'The population of sixteenth-century England rose primarily because of a fall in the death rate caused by a decline in the number and intensity of outbreaks of plague.' How far do you agree with this judgement?
6. Is it valid to claim that 'the price rise in sixteenth-century England was a result of the increase in population'?

First of all, identify the issue or issues to which each of the questions relates. Think carefully about question 1, which is not as straightforward as it may seem. Question 3 is even more difficult to assign, and there may be more than one 'correct' answer.

Look at question 5. Your first task is to 'unpack' the quotation by separating it into its component parts. There are three worth identifying. The first is the least important to you. It is the assumption that the English population rose in the sixteenth century. You will gain credit if, in your answer, you provide evidence that this was so, although it will not be a major blunder if you do not. What are the other two major components of the quotation?

Your second task is to identify what the examiner is asking you to do. In this case you are being invited to write a standard 'how far' essay – but with a difference. You will need two pairs of 'to this extent *yes*, and to this extent *no*' sections rather than the normal one. You may have noticed that question 6 is of the usual type, with just one pair of sections required.

If you feel like a real challenge, try to draw up an essay plan for question 3. Once you have replaced the first three words with a single one that means the same thing your task will be considerably simplified – but it will still be demanding. You will gain most from this exercise if you are able to compare your plan with those drawn up by others and to discuss with them the reasons for any similarities and differences.

Source-based questions on 'Population, Inflation and the Standard of Living'

1 Supply of Corn

Carefully read the extracts from the Norfolk JPs' letter of 11 July 1586 and the Act of 1597–8, given on pages 26–7. Answer the following questions.

a) Why were the Norfolk JPs writing to the Privy Council? Read the next question before answering this. *(2 marks)*

b) Summarise in one sentence the main point made by the JPs. *(2 marks)*

c) What can be deduced from the JPs' letter about the instructions they had received from the Privy Council? *(4 marks)*

d) What can be deduced from the extract from the Act of Parliament about the government's motives in proposing it? *(4 marks)*

e) What do the two extracts suggest was the government's perception of its responsibility for ensuring an adequate supply of corn throughout the country? Explain your answer. *(4 marks)*

f) For what reasons was the Act of 1597–9 unlikely to have much practical effect? *(4 marks)*

CHAPTER 3

The Economy: Agriculture and Industry

1 Introduction: Interpretations

Although many historians acknowledge the significance of demographic
fluctuations in the process of change, others attach even greater
importance to the economy. For them changes in industry and
agriculture and the expansion of wage labour are of prime importance.
Such developments, together with increasing commercialisation and
specialisation, are seen as progression towards the nineteenth-century
Industrial Revolution. Equally, much greater attention is being given to
diversity and the causes of economic growth in sixteenth-century
England. However, there is little agreement among economic
historians, who have their own interpretations of the nature and
significance of the events taking place.

* Marxist historians continue to place considerable emphasis on their
interpretation of the fourteenth-century crisis (see page 6). This they
see as creating a complete change in working relationships, with the
former peasantry being replaced by a wage labour force. Orthodox
Marxist historians regard the commercialisation of agriculture as the
prime cause of such a change. They see the growth of capitalistic
farming from the fifteenth century as creating a new, exploitative,
entrepreneurial class of landowners. By using their political power they
are considered to have driven the peasantry from the land through
enclosure and the systematic raising of rents. This new bourgeois class
of gentry and yeomen (see page 39) thus effectively gained possession of
the land and so are seen as controlling both the means and the mode of
production. The former peasantry, having lost possession of the land,
were thus forced to work for wages on the commercial farms, or in
industry, creating the new employer-employee relationship. This process is seen as leading to the creation of the landless proletariat
necessary for industrialisation in the eighteenth and nineteenth centuries.

Other Marxist historians, while agreeing in broad terms with the
orthodox approach, consider the commercialisation of industry to have
been more important. For them the emergence of the rural English
textile industry in the thirteenth century is of prime importance. They
consider that rural industry had always been an essential part of any
peasant society. Because of the seasonal nature of farming and the need
to pay rents, taxes and tithes, most peasant families are thought to have
spent part of the year working in some form of small-scale industry. For

some Marxist historians the development of a large-scale rural cloth industry (see page 44) marked the beginning of capitalistic organisation. They consider that, although the industry was based on part-time work carried out in the homes of rural workers, the actual production was in the hands of capitalistic employers – the clothiers. Moreover, large quantities of cloth were manufactured for sale abroad, and not just for local markets. This, it is considered, made it a highly capitalistic enterprise. Such a process has come to be known as 'proto-industrialisation', and is regarded by its exponents as central to any long-term explanation of the Industrial Revolution. It is considered that the first stage of industrialisation was cottage industry. The new form of production was based on family labour using more efficient machines, such as larger weaving looms and knitting frames. The proto-industrial family was largely dependent on the income of its members through such work, and so became a form of industrial proletariat. By the end of the eighteenth century this process is seen as leading to full-blown industrialisation. By then larger power-driven machinery had to be housed in highly capital intensive factories, so separating the place of work from the home. This meant that the former cottage artisans became a genuine industrial proletariat, working for wages in the factories.

    * Many economic historians are not convinced by these Marxist interpretations and are particularly sceptical about the theory of proto-industrialisation. There is widespread agreement about the underlying potential in both agriculture and industry, but there is considerable disagreement about their respective importance. In the 1960s some support was given to the idea that there were revolutions in both agriculture and industry in the late sixteenth century. Such views are no longer widely held. However, there is still considerable debate over whether the structural changes taking place in the economy were revolutionary or evolutionary. Both schools of thought recognise the long-term nature of economic development. Those historians who favour a revolutionary explanation see the economy advancing in a series of well marked leaps forward created by technological break-throughs. Evolutionists consider that change was almost imperceptible because it was governed by constant, but almost undiscernible, technical improvement. Another issue over which there is considerable controversy is whether light or heavy industry had the greatest impact in Tudor England. On one side it is maintained that most industrial activity during the century was based on the use of agricultural raw materials, such as wool or leather. However, other historians maintain that the expansion in coal production, mining and metal working with capital-intensive fixed plant, such as furnaces and forges, was more significant.

    While it is agreed that capitalism, in one form or another, was being established in Tudor England, there is a great deal of debate as to its origins. Some historians consider that rural commercialisation emerging out of the fourteenth-century crisis was of prime importance. Others argue that capitalism and wage relationships were basically urban in origin, and that commercialisation was spread by merchants and traders buying country estates or setting up rural industries. Another view is that urbanisation and the expansion of urban populations created market demand, which in turn promoted specialisation and capitalism. Equally, the theory put forward at the beginning of the twentieth century that there was a strong link between capitalism and protestantism still has its supporters. They consider that the protestant 'work ethic', with its strong emphasis on thrift, hard work and sobriety, was fundamental to the spread of capitalism. The English Reformation is seen as allowing the development of a commercial bourgeoisie drawing its members from both town and countryside. While it is agreed that the Reformation probably created a more favourable atmosphere for commercialisation by ending the medieval Church's objection to money-making, most historians now find it difficult to make a more positive linkage. There is little evidence to suggest that English Catholics were any less enterprising than Protestants, nor that commercial groups were any more capitalistically inclined than any other section of society.

* A major concern among economic historians is to try to measure the amount of economic growth discernible in Tudor England. Unfortunately the absence of reliable statistics (see page 4) and the primitive nature of sixteenth-century book-keeping and accounting make this very difficult. For the same reason attempts to measure the balance between internal and overseas trade (see page 70) is equally problematical. One method used by economic historians to measure levels of growth is to study the changing balance of people and employment in the economy. For this purpose the economy is divided into a number of sectors and the movement of people between the sectors is used to calculate whether it was becoming more or less advanced. Primitive economies are regarded as being those in which the majority of the population is engaged in low-level economic occupations, such as agriculture, fishing and forestry. Before such an economy can be seen to be advancing there has to be a marked movement of people into more advanced sectors, such as manufacturing and service industries. Although this sounds an easy way to measure economic growth, it is very difficult to use when studying sixteenth-century England because most people had more than one occupation. It is certainly true that large numbers of people were leaving farming altogether and moving into the towns, and that others were spending more time working in rural industries. The problem is in deciding whether this represented economic advance. The fact that 5 per cent more people were living in towns in 1600 than in 1500 certainly seems to indicate such progress. Furthermore, except in famine years, English agriculture appears to

have been able to feed this additional urban population. At the same time the production of textiles and leather goods expanded, which seems to indicate that English farmers not only grew more food but managed to provide the raw materials for this industrial growth. However, the majority of the rural industrial workforce was employed part-time, and only a small number of people were engaged in heavy industry by 1600. Moreover, the high levels of vagrancy and unemployment at the end of the century indicate that industry was unable to absorb the surplus labour force created by population growth and migration from the land.

* Another indicator of economic growth is thought to be productivity. It is evident that agriculture was producing more foodstuffs and raw materials from less land and with a smaller workforce, so releasing labour to work in industry. On the other hand, not enough grain was being grown to reduce living costs and so create the demand for consumer goods which was needed to promote economic growth. In any case, the capital needed to improve agriculture reduced the amount of investment available for other parts of the economy. English industry was extremely backward in comparison with that on the continent, and most of the technological advances made during the century were imported from abroad. This is considered to indicate a lack of English native enterprise at this stage. The textile trades in France, the Netherlands and Italy were much more sophisticated than their English counterparts. In terms of mining and heavy industry England lagged far behind France and, particularly, Germany. By comparison Tudor industry is regarded as being small-scale and labour intensive, with low productivity. As a result England remained heavily dependent on imported manufactured goods during the sixteenth century. The lack of positive signs of either growth or increased productivity have caused many historians to conclude that the Tudor economy was not very dynamic. They consider that the sixteenth century was a period when England was catching up with continental technology and laying the foundations for future growth.

2 The Commercialisation of Farming

Whichever of the theoretical interpretations is adopted, it is generally agreed that commercial farming had become firmly established in most parts of England by 1600. This does not mean that peasant agriculture had totally disappeared or that farming in some form did not continue to be the main occupation of the majority of the population. However, general, mixed farming by smallholders to produce food for their own family consumption was becoming rarer. Even husbandmen with quite modestly sized farms appear to have been very market-orientated and willing to specialise their production. This is not to say that commercial farming was new. During the middle ages the aristocracy and the monasteries had used their demesnes (those parts of their estates that were not rented out) for the large-scale production of foodstuffs and wool. Although much of the work had been done by the peasantry in the form of labour services, additional wage labourers had been frequently employed. At the same time peasant smallholders grew some crops for sale in order to raise money to pay rents and other dues, and had been just as keen to make a profit as were their Tudor counterparts. Similarly, industrial crops, such as saffron (for dyes and spices) and hemp (for rope making), were grown in the middle ages, and enclosure (see page 39) was a common farming practice. What was new was that the changes in the fourteenth century and the virtual disappearance of serfdom had created a freer and more mobile society that was more atuned to market demand. This, it is suggested, enabled the development of larger and more efficient farms by the gentry, yeomen and some husbandmen. Commercialisation was helped by enclosure, which brought additional good land and previously unproductive commons under more intensive cultivation. In turn these two developments enabled the introduction of new techniques and crops (see page 40). The overall result was to create greater specialisation, diversification and the emergence of a variety of farming regions.

   * It has been suggested that one of the most significant changes in agriculture in sixteenth-century England was the reduction of inefficient, small-scale peasant farming. This, it is considered, not only enabled more effective use to be made of the land, but also, by reducing self-sufficiency, created greater market demand. A major problem with peasant farming is the necessity to grow a variety of crops to meet the needs of family consumption. Medieval over-population, which had led to the settlement and arable farming of poor quality marginal grassland, had made the situation worse. In addition it is thought that this created an imbalance between arable and grazing land. This meant that insufficient livestock could be kept to produce the manure needed to revitalise the soil. The result was the over-cropping of soils, which were frequently unsuitable for this type of general cultivation. Furthermore, the problem was compounded by the inefficient three-course crop rotation used in many open field systems where one field was left fallow every year. This gave insufficient time for the soil to renew itself and caused soil exhaustion leading to a steady decrease in crop yields. With the onset of poor weather conditions in the thirteenth century it is not hard to understand why late medieval farming is thought to have been incapable of feeding the estimated population of six million in 1300. The strong demographic downturn between 1350 and 1450 allowed the reversion of the more marginal land back to pasture, so helping to restore the balance between arable and grazing land.

   * A major consequence of this shift in balance is considered to be the emergence of larger farms, the replacement of peasant agriculture and a reduction in the levels of self-sufficiency. Peasant smallholdings had

characteristically been between 10 and 40 acres in size; small enough to be worked by family labour, while providing enough food to support the family unit. The new commercial farms were generally over 100 acres and worked by wage labour. The gentry, and later the aristocracy, when they had ceased to be encumbered by long leases, divided their estates into larger farms by putting together several former smallholdings. These were generally let as copyhold, or leasehold (see page 102) for terms of up to 20 years. Those landowners with estates adjacent to expanding town markets frequently ran their own demesnes as commercial undertakings. At the same time many husbandmen were able to enlarge their farms by taking over vacant plots (known as engrossing), until the increasing population put pressure back on the land after the 1560s. This increased the number of yeomen, who by accumulating parcels of freehold, leasehold and copyhold land could create quite large farms, which put them economically on a par with many of the gentry. However, it is clear that the creation of large farms was a very uneven process which was most pronounced in south-east England. In some parts of the country traditional farming continued unchanged, and often individual villages remained unaffected while those around them were commercialised.

This was equally true with enclosure, which is seen as an integral part of commercialisation. Much of the late fifteenth and early sixteenth-century enclosure is thought to have been for the creation of large sheep runs on land that had reverted back to pasture. In 1517 a commission found that rents for pasture were 40 per cent higher than for arable land. This reflects the high price of wool over the first half of the sixteenth century. At the time, large-scale enclosure of this type was condemned because it was thought to drive people off the land and to create depopulation. However, not all enclosure was of this sort. John Fitzherbert, the agriculturalist, writing in the 1520s considered that enclosed land was excellent for both arable and stock farming. Landowners were keen to fence off their enlarged farms because enclosed land commanded higher rents (see page 23). Many of the yeomen and husbandmen enclosed their land which they had consolidated from the open fields, while others were content to leave their land scattered (see page 41). Enclosed arable land was considered to be more efficient to manage and as giving greater flexibility in the choice and rotation of crops. It was equally useful for stock raising, giving greater scope for experimentation and selective breeding. The 1517 commission found that in Berkshire 60 per cent of land that had been enclosed was used for arable. Another commission in 1548 stated that the bad type of enclosure was that of commonland. This was considered to be the major cause of depopulation, because the fencing of commons for private use or their division to create or to add to commercial farms, deprived the villagers of access. Without the use of common land for such things as grazing their animals, collecting firewood or gathering wild fruit, cottagers were often plunged into poverty, and many were forced to leave their homes in order to find alternative employment. For this reason, although only some 2 per cent of new land was fenced off, enclosure was a major issue in Tudor England. Not only was it a cause of popular discontent, but the government, fearing vagrancy and social instability, constantly legislated against the practice. Even so, many economic historians regard enclosure as a major contributor to agricultural improvement and specialisation.

3 An Agricultural Revolution?

The increase in commercialisation and specialisation led E. Kerridge to the claim in the 1960s that there was a sixteenth-century agricultural revolution. Apart from the spread of commercial farming, it is maintained that the introduction of new techniques and crops marked a noticeable advance in English agriculture. This, it is thought, enabled more food to be produced from less land by a smaller workforce. Those supporting the idea of an agricultural revolution stress that the use of enclosures and new methods of crop rotation were fundamental to agricultural progress. The most important break-through is considered to have been a new system of rotation called 'up and down husbandry'. In the old open field system one of the three great arable fields was left fallow under pasture every year to recover fertility. Under the new method enclosed land was used as arable for a number of years, and then for pasture for a similar period. This technique is considered to have maintained a better balance between arable and grazing land and to have prevented soil exhaustion. Moreover, it is claimed that up and down husbandry was four times more efficient than the open field method. In addition, grazing land was improved by the use of floating water meadows; a technique by which river side meadows were flooded annually through sluices so that the river silt would improve the quality of the grass. Animal feed was improved by the introduction of fodder crops, such as clover and lucerne. Because of these advances, and the use of enclosures, individual farmers were able to separate their cattle and sheep from the village herds and flocks on the commons. This enabled them to improve the quality of their animals by selective breeding. Furthermore, more industrial crops, such as saffron and woad for dyeing, rapeseed for oil, hops for brewing and flax and hemp for linen and cordage, were being grown. In total, it is claimed, such changes were revolutionary.

Many historians do not find this argument convincing. It is agreed that all these innovations were taking place, but the pace at which they were being adopted is not considered rapid enough to amount to a revolution. Although some books, such as John Fitzherbert's *Book of Husbandry* of 1523, were being published, the level of literacy among even the gentry is not thought to have been great enough for many farmers to have read them. In any case the spread of new techniques is thought to have been very patchy. The level of return on the capital costs is not felt to have been high enough to encourage large-scale investment except for sheep runs. Only landowners and farmers living close to expanding towns, especially London, are considered to have had sufficient incentive to undertake extensive improvements of arable land. Indeed, it is considered that most farmers were content to enclose land for grazing and avoid the higher costs of improving arable cultivation. Contemporary opinion seems to agree with this view.

An Act Concerning Farms and Sheep, 1533/4

1 [Various wealthy people] . . . have daily studied practices and invented ways and means how they might accumulate and gather together into a few hands as well great multitude of farms as great plenty of cattle and in especially sheep, putting such lands as they
5 can get to pasture and not to tillage . . . and [the reason why they] keep in their hands such great portions of the grounds of this realm from [the] occupying of the poor husbandmen, and so to use it in pasture and not in tillage, is only the great profit that cometh of sheep. . .

The Commonwealth of this Realm of England, 1549

1 . . . Our profits was but small by the ploughs, therefore divers [many] of my neighbours . . . [have] turned either part or all their arable land into pasture, and thereby have waxed [grown] very rich men. And every day some of us enclose a [plot] of his ground
5 to pasture; and were it not that our ground lieth in the commonfields, intermingled one with another, I think also our fields had been enclosed, of a common agreement of all the township, [village] long ere this time. And to say the truth I have enclosed or nothing of my ground [but because of] a little breed of neat
10 [cattle], sheep, swine, geese, and hens that I do rear on my ground; whereof because the price is somewhat round [high], I make more clear profit than I do of all my corn.

The act of 1597 (see page 26) suggests that this problem remained unresolved at the end of the century. This seems to support the pessimistic view that, far from being revolutionary, Tudor agriculture was barely able to produce enough grain to keep pace with population growth.

    * Most historians, while agreeing that agricultural performance was not dynamic, consider that the problems of the 1590s had more to do with the particularly bad weather than with any fundamental faults in production methods. It is thought that by the end of the century new techniques and crops were being more widely adopted. Nevertheless, it

is admitted that, even during periods of good weather, Tudor farmers did not succeed in significantly reducing the price of grain and thereby off-setting the effects of inflation. This, it is felt, was not achieved until the seventeenth century. However, some historians feel that this is too optimistic a view, and that no real agricultural advance was made until the eighteenth century. In any case, it is not until quite recently that historians even considered that agriculture had any impact on economic growth. It is now agreed that profits from agriculture could create demand, although there is debate whether or not the apparently increased incomes of the farming sector were not largely absorbed by inflation. Indeed, it has been suggested that any increased income was invested in better houses and a more comfortable lifestyle rather than in the economy. Furthermore, it is pointed out that, apart from money required to introduce new techniques and create enclosures, very large sums of capital were absorbed into the barns, mills and other fixed buildings needed by the farmer. This is seen to mean that, although agriculture was successfully shedding its workforce, there was insufficient remaining capital to invest in new industries to absorb the surplus labour. Another problem, it is suggested, was that land could not be used for both agricultural and industrial purposes at the same time. If more foodstuffs were being produced then there was less land available to produce timber, hides, wool and industrial crops, or for activities such as mining. A further difficulty faced by both farmers and industrialists was one of distribution, and until there had been a marked improvement in England's transport system (see chapter 4) economic prospects seemed poor.

Such considerations make it hard to come to any firm conclusions about agricultural performance in Tudor England. It seems that even by 1600 there were still problems in feeding the expanding population in years when the weather was bad, although this did not amount to the previously suggested subsistence crises. Poor communications may have hindered the development of specialist farming areas and inter-regional exchanges. However, the exceedingly rapid expansion of London did lead to an improvement of road and river transport in the Home Counties to help to supply the capital's food markets. A major problem appears to have been the high price of wool and other animal products which discouraged the growing of cereals. Tudor governments at the end of the century were just as concerned as those at the beginning to encourage husbandmen to return to arable farming to produce more grain.

4 The Nature of Tudor Industry

It must be remembered that there was no clear-cut division between industry and agriculture in Tudor England. The seasonal nature of farming meant that during slack periods in the agricultural year most

people were engaged in other occupations. This dual economy extended
to all sections of society. Large numbers of the lower orders were
engaged in some form of cottage industry, mainly related to textiles or
leather. At peak farming periods, such as harvesting, urban industries
largely closed down, and the poorer sections of town society went to
work on the neighbouring farms. The increasingly large numbers of
young vagrants were only too pleased to find work in either agriculture
or industry whenever it was available. Yeomen and husbandmen
frequently engaged in several other activities, such as inn keeping,
shipbuilding, mining or tanning, as well as farming. Indeed, it is often
difficult to tell from their inventories just what was their main
occupation. Titles were inter-changeable: an individual might at some
times be called a yeomen, and at others a shoemaker or a butcher. Such
diversity of activity, on a larger scale, was just as common among the
gentry and aristocracy. The iron masters of Sussex were largely drawn
from local gentry and yeomen families, while many of the larger coal
and metal working enterprises were sponsored by members of the
aristocracy.

All historians are agreed as to the importance of this inter-
relationship. Clearly the transfer of labour from farming to industry is a
central issue in the debate over economic growth. Of equal importance
was the ability of agriculture to feed the growing proportion of the
population that was becoming increasingly dependent on the market for
its food supply. This raises the issue as to whether, even if agriculture
was producing the required amounts of food, it could at the same time
supply the raw materials and land needed by industry to expand. Tudor
manufacturing was still based on wool and leather, and both the textile
and leather trades needed other industrial crops, such as saffron or
woad for dyes. The relationship between town and countryside was
highly important. As industrial centres, towns were major consumers of
food and raw materials drawn from the countryside. At the same time,
the authorities feared that competition from rural industry would
adversely effect urban production and cause unemployment and rioting. For this reason Tudor governments tried to encourage the
expansion of industry in the towns, and to restrict the spread of rural
manufacturing. The Act of Artificers in 1563 was an attempt to ensure
that industries were only established by craftsmen who had served a
seven year apprenticeship. This, it was hoped, would prevent unqualified gentry, yeomen and husbandmen from setting up new industries
in the countryside. This problem was made worse by the arrival of
skilled continental migrants, which was a major concern among urban
authorities who saw them as constituting unfair competition for their
own craftsmen. For some historians this problem was great enough to
constitute an 'urban crisis'. Others consider that the real crisis was the
inability of many towns to employ, feed or house the influx of unskilled
labour from the countryside. However, the growth of urban demand

can be seen as a major driving force towards economic growth. On the other hand, if agriculture was unable to provide sufficient quantities of cheap food, demand for consumer goods would remain small, and so industrial growth would be restricted.

* Apart from debates over the balance between industry and agriculture, historians are divided over what type of industrial development was most significant in the Tudor economy. Those historians supporting the idea of a large-scale, rural textile industry leading eventually to the Industrial Revolution, clearly stress the importance of cottage industry. They regard the conflict between urban and rural industry as being part of the struggle between the 'feudal', small-scale, craft industries of the towns and the capitalistic large-scale production of the countryside. Other historians see the expansion and diversification of craft industries based on agricultural raw materials, in both town and country, as a major feature of the Tudor economy. Another school of thought supports the importance of heavy industry with capital-intensive fixed plant, although there is disagreement about whether this should be regarded as a revolution. On the other hand, a number of historians consider the introduction and spread of highly capitalistic industries, such as paper and glass making, as highly significant. It is unlikely that there will ever be any agreement among the advocates of any of these interpretations as to whether industrial growth in the sixteenth century was evolutionary or revolutionary, or to what extent any expansion was dependent upon continental technology and expertise.

5 Changes in the Manufacture of Textiles

During most of the middle ages the English textile industry had been confined to the towns, and organised by the guilds. Each part of the manufacturing process – carding, combing, spinning and weaving – had its own craft guild, as did the finishing trades of fulling, shearing, napping and dyeing. At the end of each stage, the product was sold on to craftsmen concerned in the next process of manufacture. The finished cloth was then sold at wholesale price to another group of guild members, taylors, mercers and merchants, either for local retail sale or for export abroad. Individual master craftsmen, who had served a seven year apprenticeship, operated in their own homes under regulations laid down by their guild. They could train new apprentices, who lived with them as part of their family, and employ journeymen or day workers. These journeymen had served their apprenticeship but had to work for wages until they had saved enough money to set themselves up independently in business (see page 19).

Then, in the thirteenth century, many master craftsmen left the towns to establish the textile industry in the countryside, and became known as clothiers. Historians are divided over the relative importance of the various causes of this movement that have been identified. However, it is generally agreed that the main reasons were to take advantage of cheaper rural wage rates, to escape guild restrictions and to avoid the high urban cost of living. This development established the two rival forms of textile manufacture that existed in England throughout the sixteenth century. The urban guild manufacture had a small, skilled workforce, and produced small quantities of expensive finished cloth. In contrast, in the rural industry there was a large, part-time, semi-skilled, labour force, making considerable amounts of cheaper, semi-finished textiles. Those historians who see this as an important step towards capitalism point out that it transformed England from a mere source of raw materials, into a country exporting sizeable quantities of semi-manufactured goods (see page 58). The new industry was free of guild restrictions. The labour force was initially self-employed, worked at home using their own equipment, such as looms and spinning wheels, and were paid by the clothiers for the cloth or yarn they produced. However, the rising cost of materials during the sixteenth century gradually forced increasing numbers of cottage workers into working for wages and giving up their independence in an attempt to maintain their standard of living.

Apart from agriculture, rural textile manufacture became the largest single employer, particularly of women, in England. It was organised on a capitalistic basis by the clothiers who bought raw wool and distributed it for carding, combing and spinning among their cottage workers. This 'putting out' system was completed by the clothier distributing the resultant yarn to weavers. Generally they worked in their own homes and were paid on a piece-work basis. Completed cloths were collected by the clothier to be fulled (beaten in water and clay to thicken and clean them) at his mill. The resultant 'white' or 'unfinished' cloth was mainly sold abroad, generally through the Merchant Adventurers Company to the Netherlands (see page 59). Unlike the urban industry, the quality of finishing in the countryside was not considered good enough to meet continental standards. For this reason the 'white' cloth was sent to the Netherlands for finishing and resale.

The virtually unrestricted nature of the rural industry until 1563 meant that anyone with sufficient capital could become a clothier. During the early sixteenth century many clothiers, such as Thomas Spring of Lavenham (see page 89), made considerable fortunes, and in several cases their descendants became members of the gentry. Government attempts to place restrictions on their activities culminated in the Act of Artificers. Among its many clauses was one which made it illegal for anyone who had not served an apprenticeship to set themselves up as a clothier, or to employ anyone with a similar qualification. In part this was in response to guild complaints of shoddy workmanship in the rural industry. At the same time it was an attempt to force more people into apprenticeship and training so as to build up a skilled workforce which could compete with the continental industries. Although it did eventually limit the number of totally unqualified clothiers in the industry, the provisions of the Act were not widely enforced in the countryside (see page 52).

* Until the 1560s the main product of the rural industry was a heavy wool cloth, known as the 'old draperies'. The major areas of production were East Anglia, Essex, the West Country and the East and West Ridings of Yorkshire, although some cloth was produced in almost every county. Various types of cloth were manufactured, ranging from the fine worsteds made in Norfolk and the heavy broadcloths of Essex and the West Country, to smaller, lighter kerseys and fustians from Suffolk and Lancashire. Demand for English textiles in the Netherlands seemed insatiable until the 1550s, when the Antwerp cloth market began to decline. Then exports fell and recession hit many of the clothmaking areas. The main reason for the slump was that heavy woollen cloth was going out of fashion on the continent. A lighter fabric, in which wool was mixed with cotton, linen or silk, was becoming more favoured. By the 1550s the textile industries in France and the Netherlands had responded to this change and were beginning to make lighter cloths, known as the 'new draperies'. During the second half of the sixteenth century the English textile industry in both town and country had to come to terms with this development. In doing this England was helped by the religious persecution of Protestants in the Netherlands and France. Many skilled continental clothworkers fled from this repression, hoping to find refuge in England. They settled in large numbers in Kent, Essex and East Anglia, bringing with them the new techniques. By the end of the century the 'new draperies' had become well established, particularly in Norfolk, where the lighter bays, says and 'Norwich stuffs', were being produced. From the 1590s wool prices were rising rapidly, showing that production was increasing again. However, two major problems remained. The quality of English finishing was still inferior, despite the fact that there had been improvements in dyeing helped by the increased growing of woad, saffron and oil seed rape. At the same time it was necessary for English merchants to open up new markets to replace the one lost in the Netherlands, and this was not to be achieved fully until the next century. Even so textiles were still England's only major manufactured export in 1600.

6 The Smaller Craft, Cottage and Capitalistic Enterprises

Apart from the major production of textiles, a wide range of manufacturing was carried out in the craft and small capitalistic enterprises to be found all over England. They operated in every urban centre down to the smallest market town, and in many villages. As in the case of textiles, they could be run by craftsmen of all sorts, as well as by gentry, yeomen and husbandmen. Equally, the employees ranged from the full-time, highly skilled to part-time casual labour. The majority of these occupations were carried out in the home of the employer. Larger operators might have a workshop, sometimes a converted monastic building, adjacent to their premises and employ additional labour. Other employers adopted a more capitalistic approach and operated small putting-out systems in the neighbouring villages. The great majority of these handicrafts used agricultural raw materials. However, there were silversmiths, plumbers, glaziers or nailmakers, as well as saddlers, glovers, shoemakers and carpenters. Most of these industries were traditional, producing on a small scale and generally for sale on the premises or at the local markets.

From the 1560s this type of industrial activity began to show greater diversification. The reason for this was the introduction of new skills and techniques by refugees from the continent. This trend was encouraged by the government. Under Elizabeth I, William Cecil, Lord Burghley, maintained a consistent policy of promoting full employment through introducing new industries from the continent. This was not a new idea, as in 1549 Sir Thomas Smith had commented that in Italy 'they reward and cherish every man that brings in any new art or mystery whereby the people may be set to work'. Burghley's approach was to increase the number of patents issued to foreigners with particular skills to allow them to settle and operate freely in England. In addition they were given a monopoly protecting the production and sale of their manufacture for periods of up to 20 years. As a result of this policy a number of new industries besides the 'new draperies' became established in England. In the 1570s French emigrants were allowed to settle in Spittlefields, in London, to set up silk weaving, and this later moved to Sudbury in Suffolk. During the same period stocking knitting and lace making were introduced and spread to become important cottage industries in various parts of the country. Linen weavers settled in several places in the south-east, and this encouraged the growing of flax as an industrial crop. Even the Elizabethan liking for elaborate ruffs encouraged new enterprise, as many continental starch makers settled in London to meet the demands of the fashion. However, these handicraft industries were not on a large scale, and they produced insufficient quantities of manufactures to supply more than the internal market. Thus, although they did help to provide employment and increase technical skills, they did nothing to increase exports.

* A major concern of the government was to reduce England's dependence on continental industry for metalwares and other technically advanced products, such as paper and glass. To this end the patent system was used to encourage larger, capitalistically financed enterprises. A good example of this policy was in the manufacture of good quality window glass, which was in high demand because of the

extensive building of larger and more comfortable houses by the elites. In 1562 Jean Carre, a Netherlander, was given a patent to manufacture glass in England. He succeeded in producing large quantities of cheap, high quality window glass. After his death in 1572 his techniques were adopted by a number of English glass makers, who had previously concentrated on producing bottle glass. Many patents were issued during the last part of the century to a variety of capitalistic enterprises, with the aim of establishing completely new processes. Particular attention was paid to the production of industrial chemicals, such as alum, for paper making, dyeing and tanning, or saltpetre for the manufacture of gunpowder. Great interest was shown in mining and metallurgy. A number of patents were issued to German experts, such as the German Mining Company set up in Cumberland to extract copper. Other patents were given to such enterprises as paper making, wire drawing, brewing and nail making. The building trades were expanded through the large-scale production of bricks and tiles. Unfortunately, although this all helped with the process of catching up with continental technology, production levels were low. This meant that costs were high and that it was often cheaper to import goods from the continent. Although the use of patents had helped to introduce new technology and skills into the economy, some historians consider that the granting of such monopolies slowed down industrial growth by preventing competition.

7 Mining and Heavy Industry

There is still much debate about the importance of mining and heavy industry in the Tudor economy, and whether it was, as once thought, revolutionary. In the 1930s J.U. Nef suggested that there was a Tudor industrial revolution centred on this sector. This idea was based on the assumption that there was a timber crisis in the sixteenth century which meant that increasing quantities of coal were being used for domestic and industrial purposes. This, it was claimed, caused considerable expansion in coal extraction, which was helped by the closure of the monasteries because the new owners of monastic estates were able to exploit coal and mineral deposits ignored by the monks. It was suggested that three key areas in the economy – shipbuilding, salt extraction and glass manufacturing – benefited from the increased use of coal. Shipbuilding expanded through the need to transport coal, while the use of the new fuel enabled the other two industries to develop. Few historians currently accept this interpretation. It is now felt that any shortages of timber and charcoal were purely local. Certainly more coal was being used domestically, especially 'sea coal', so called because it was shipped from Newcastle to London. Coal was also beginning to be used in industries, such as salt extraction, lime burning and brick making. However, it is not thought such industries were sufficiently important, or that enough coal was being used by 1600 to amount to a revolution. In any case, it is suggested, backward technology, poor transport facilities and lack of investment meant that the coal industry did not expand significantly until the seventeenth century. Problems of ventilation and drainage meant that coal was mined mainly by open cast methods or from shallow bell pits. Although coal was mined in the Weald, the Forest of Dean, Northumberland, Lancashire, the Midlands and parts of Wales (see map below), these were small-scale operations and the coal produced was used only locally.

* Similar doubts have been expressed about the importance of mineral mining and metallurgy. It has been pointed out that it was not until the eighteenth century that charcoal was successfully replaced by

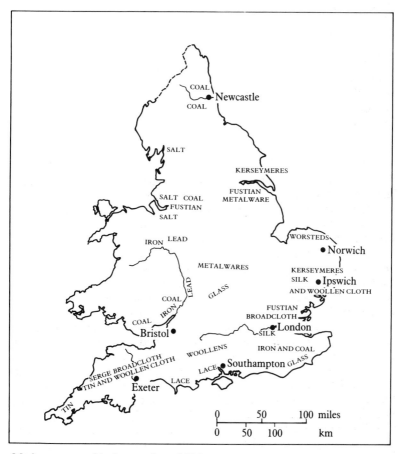

Main centres of industry circa 1600

coal for smelting iron ore. Likewise, coal was not used in glass manufacture, or metal vats utilised for salt evaporation until the seventeenth century. The major centre for iron production continued to be the Weald in Sussex. At the end of the fifteenth century the gentry and yeoman ironmasters had adopted a new type of blast furnace from the continent. These furnaces, which had water-driven bellows, were fuelled by charcoal and were particularly useful in producing the cast iron needed for making cannons. During the early sixteenth century England was reliant on France for cast iron and good quality cannons. The first cast iron cannon was produced in the Weald in 1543. By 1570 the number of furnaces in the area had risen from 26 to over 100, and England was becoming independent in the manufacture of cannon. However, the Wealden and other iron processing areas were small scale and out-put was low. Moreover, the iron ore was of poor quality and production was dependent on imported higher grade Swedish ore. Most English iron ore was made into pig iron, which was converted into bar iron in finery forges. The iron bars were distributed to blacksmiths and other metalworkers to make into tools and other items. Although the metal trades around Birmingham and Dudley were expanding, growth was hampered by transport difficulties. Many roads were still unsuitable for wheeled vehicles and even the major rivers were navigable only over short stretches (see page 71). Consequently, iron ore had to be carried by pack animals. This was a slow process which meant that distribution continued to be very localised.

Other types of heavy industry, although expanding and diversifying, remained on a small scale. Production from the Cornish tins mines fluctuated, but was helped by increased domestic demand. Silver, pewter (an alloy of lead and tin) and brass (an alloy of lead, tin and zinc) were becoming increasingly popular among the wealthier sections of society. This encouraged increased activity in lead and zinc mining in the Mendips and Shropshire and the introduction of new technology, such as a more advanced blast furnace for lead smelting. However, like iron, such operations were capital intensive. In the 1580s it was estimated that it cost £824 to set up an iron furnace. This made them a high risk at a time when profits were relatively modest. At the same time they needed only a small skilled workforce, with extra casual labour being employed at busy times, so providing few openings for the unskilled unemployed. Consequently, this sector, although expanding and forming the basis for growth, did not have a really significant impact on the Tudor economy.

8 Conclusion

It is very difficult to draw any firm conclusions about the industrial sector as a whole. There is general agreement that there was not an industrial revolution in the late sixteenth century. Indeed, the overall

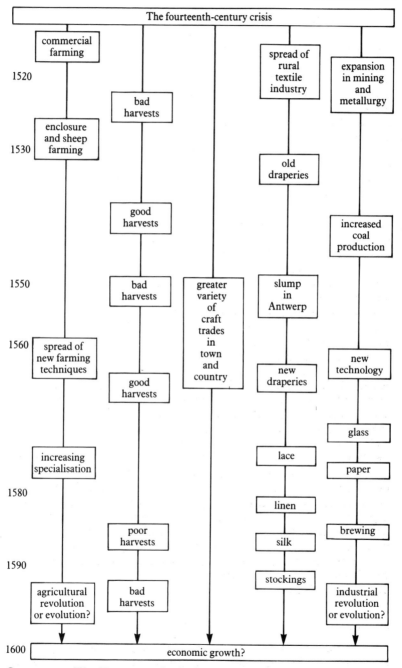

Summary – The Economy: Agriculture and Industry

impression is of great underlying continuity, marked by some technological improvement. This is seen as part of the process of catching up with the technically advanced continent. Significant advance is considered to have been very haphazard. Government intervention through legislation and the patent system does not appear to have had much impact by 1600. Many of the new enterprises were very expensive and did little to provide more employment. Moreover, it is considered that, although some advance was made in becoming less dependent on foreign manufactures, many of the new English products were more expensive than the competing imports. Textiles remained the only major industry and the sole manufactured export. Otherwise, industrial activity is seen as being a mixture of handicrafts and small capitalistic enterprises, with low production and employment capabilities. However, it is thought that much of the seemingly unproductive investment was highly important in laying the basis for future growth in the next century. Neither the agricultural nor the industrial sectors seem to have been very dynamic by 1600. Although the government increased its efforts to gain greater control over the economy after 1558, it had little success. The main reason for this was that central authority was still limited. Governmment legislation was frequently modified to such an extent in parliament that it was virtually inoperable. In any case, landowners and industrialists simply ignored any measures that they thought were against their own interests. Attempts to restrict rural industry in favour of the towns appear to have failed. However, despite this, most towns appear to have been recovering from the 'urban crisis' by the end of the century. It is estimated that by 1600 only some 250,000 people were directly dependent upon non-agricultural work for their livelihood. This suggests that industry had not been very successful in absorbing surplus labour from agriculture. Certainly the clause in the Act of Artificers, stipulating that everyone between the ages of 12 and 60, below the rank of gentry and not apprenticed in industry or trade had to become a servant in husbandry, confirms that the government was concerned about unemployment. The growing number of unemployed young vagrants and increasing levels of poverty and destitution by 1600 indicate that neither industry nor the government had solved this problem. Even so, agriculture and industry cannot be seen in isolation and must be considered in the wider context of trade and commerce.

Making notes on 'The Economy: Agriculture and Industry'

Section 1 examines the growing debate as to how Tudor agriculture and industry should be interpreted. Although it is generally agreed that capitalism in some form was spreading, there is little unity of opinion as to what form it took. To understand this debate it is essential that you have a firm grasp of the various theories and interpretations so that you can judge their strengths and weaknesses. One of the difficulties in analysing pre-industrial economies is that agriculture and industry were so closely linked. This makes it hard to use economic growth to measure performance. You should list the possible areas of growth and in each case note the problems of assessing performance before deciding where (and if) there were signs of expansion. Historians are generally agreed that pre-industrial economic change was a long-term process and that developments were evolutionary rather than revolutionary. For this reason it is helpful to think of the Tudor economy in terms of being part of a stage of transition that was to last until 1650, if not until the Industrial Revolution.

The remaining sections examine agriculture and industry in more detail. Section 2 discusses to what extent commercialisation had improved or worsened the food supply in comparison with traditional methods. You need to consider these issues very carefully. Refer to your notes on chapter 2 to help to decide why there were possible agricultural crises in 1549 and again in the 1590s. Section 3 examines the debate about whether such changes amounted to an agricultural revolution. Remember that many historians now think that by 1600 agriculture was still in a phase of evolution that was to last until the 1650s. After reading section 4 you will need to make careful notes about the general organisation of Tudor industry. Section 5 looks at developments in the main Tudor manufacturing industry. Examine the changes in the cloth industry and consider why there was an economic depression in the 1550s and again in the 1590s. Section 6 looks at the wide range of smaller industries that made up a large proportion of the Tudor industrial sector. Think carefully about changes in these other craft and capitalistic enterprises and assess why they did little to help the economy. After reading section 7 note the reasons why it was once thought that there was a revolution in Tudor heavy industry, and consider the arguments against the idea. Think carefully about the conclusions drawn in section 8 and, after you have read chapter 4, refer back to your notes on this chapter and re-assess your opinion on the success or failure of the Tudor economy.

Source-based questions on 'The Economy: Agriculture and Industry'

1 The Conversion of Arable to Pasture

Carefully read the extracts from the Act of 1533–4 and 'The Commonwealth of this Realm of England' given on page 41. Answer the following questions.

a) The writers of both extracts suggest the same reason why many farmers had turned arable land into pasture. What was this reason? (*2 marks*)

b) What evidence does the first extract contain that the framers of the Act disapproved of the conversion of arable land to pasture? Support your answer by quoting from the extract. (*3 marks*)

c) It was the assumed effects of the loss of arable land that worried most governments in Tudor England. What were these effects thought to be? (*5 marks*)

d) What explanation does the author of the second extract give for the fact that not all the land in his locality had been converted to pasture? (*2 marks*)

e) What difference in attitude towards the conversion of arable land to pasture do the two extracts reveal? Which attitude was the more influential in Tudor England? Explain your answer. (*6 marks*)

f) In what ways have historians disagreed with sixteenth-century opinions about the extent and significance of enclosure? (*7 marks*)

CHAPTER 4

The Economy: Overseas and Internal Trade

1 Introduction

Overseas trade has always attracted much attention in terms of measuring economic growth, although most historians would agree that internal trade was just as (if not more) important. The reason for this is possibly that the records of goods shipped abroad are plentiful, while statistics for inland trade are virtually non-existent. Even so, many historians consider that the data on exports is too fragmentary and open to misinterpretation (see page 4) to give any clear quantitative picture of the volume of Tudor overseas trade. In spite of this, greater importance is often attached to England's performance abroad than to the state of the domestic market. Some historians consider this to be misleading, because exports represented only a small percentage of the gross national product. In any case, it is felt that economic performance can be assessed only through studying how well both internal and external trade distributed production from the agricultural and industrial sectors.

English overseas trade in the sixteenth century is seen as falling into two distinct phases. The period up to 1550 was dominated by the sale of woollen cloth to the Netherlands. It was followed by a concerted effort to extend trade outlets in Europe and to break into world trade. To a large extent the reason for this pattern is seen to be political and diplomatic. Until the death of Mary I in 1558, Tudor foreign policy was geared very closely to Western Europe and was linked with the dynastic struggle between the Habsburg rulers of Spain and the Holy Roman Empire against France. From before 1500 England was allied with the Habsburgs against the long-standing, national enemy, France. In economic terms this was very advantageous because the great bulk of English cloth was exported to the Netherlands, which were ruled by the Habsburgs. During the 1550s the whole situation changed. The Antwerp cloth market began to break down, forcing English merchants to seek new markets. Then, in 1558, the death of Mary I effectively ended the Anglo-Habsburg alliance, and, under Elizabeth I, England's relations with the Spanish Habsburgs soon deteriorated into open warfare. The long conflict between the Habsburgs and France was concluded in 1559 because of the exhaustion and bankruptcy of both sides. Western Europe became destabilised and lapsed into a series of religious and civil wars which lasted until the end of the century. This period of weakness, it is considered, enabled England to expand her markets in Europe and to break into world trade. The Far Eastern and American markets opened up by Portugal and Spain in the fifteenth century had been divided between them by the Pope in the Treaty of Tordesillas in 1494. After 1558 Protestant England no longer felt obliged to observe this arrangement. A period of aggressive anti-Catholic foreign policy led to English merchants trying to open up markets that had previously been considered to be Spanish and Portuguese monopolies.

2 General Theories of Pre-Industrial Trade

Many historians see these developments as part of the rise of the state and the establishment of capitalism (see page 57). Economic historians used to talk of the period between the sixteenth and eighteenth centuries as a commercial revolution, when English merchants learned the skills necessary to develop a world market in which to sell the products of the Industrial Revolution. Some historians see the period as one of mercantilism. Central to this idea is the intervention in the economy by the state. Just as the government was seen to be anxious to control industry and agriculture and to encourage full employment, so it aimed to organise internal and external trade. It has been suggested that the earliest 'mercantilistic' legislation was the Statute of Labourers in 1350, which was designed to regulate wages after the Black Death. Certainly the Statute of Artificers (see page 43), which revised the earlier act and introduced new legislation, is seen as an attempt to consolidate state control over industry, employment and trade. One major concern of the government was to encourage full employment and new industries so as to make England less dependent on foreign goods. This case was argued by Sir Thomas Smith who wished to see the country independent of all imports. This, he thought, would create a favourable balance of trade and so increase the nation's wealth. In addition, the discovery of new markets would mean that more English goods would be sold abroad. Just as the government tried to encourage new industry through the patent system (see page 47), so the granting of charters and monopolies to trading companies from the 1550s is seen as an attempt to establish state control over foreign trade. Historians, such as D.C. Coleman, consider that the government needed to adopt an increasingly aggressive foreign policy in order to win new markets. Home industry and trade had to be protected by tariffs and embargoes, while seapower and wars gained England a growing share of the world market.

* A more recent interpretation of these events (see page 8) is that between 1450 and 1640 a world economic system was being created which established long-distance trade on a capitalist basis. The 'four-teenth-century crisis' is suggested as the starting point of this process. Dramatic demographic decline in Western Europe is seen as the main

cause of the recession of the fifteenth century because it caused such an enormous drop in the volume of trade. In any case, until 1450 Western European commerce is regarded as being only short-distance; between the main centres of the Baltic, the Netherlands and the Mediterranean. The only long-distance trading was in luxury goods, such as silks, spices and gems, along the overland routes through Asia from the Far East to the Eastern Mediterranean. Apart from reducing trade, the crisis is seen as creating other problems. With the reduction in the amount of arable land (see page 38), Western Europe was faced with difficulties in growing enough foodstuffs, such as wheat and sugar, and producing sufficient raw materials for industry. Moreover, as the imports from the Far East had to be paid for in silver there was an urgent need to find new supplies of bullion. These problems are seen as the driving force behind the Western European expansion, deriving from the Spanish and Portuguese voyages of discovery. The whole process is again linked with the rise of the state. Newly centralising states, such as Spain, Portugal, England and France, are considered to have been forced to expand overseas in order to meet the rising cost of government and warfare. Although Spain and Portugal were the first to open up world trade, their increasing insolvency and weakness by the end of the sixteenth century is seen as allowing the Dutch, English and French to break their monopoly of trade with the Far East and the Americas. This, it is suggested, created a capitalist world system. England, France (and later, Holland) are seen as becoming the 'core' states. Such countries were predominantly Protestant and had capitalistically organised, industrial economies based on wage labour and increasing urbanisation. The remaining Western European states, with Catholic, feudalistic, rural economies dependent upon peasant agriculture, formed a 'semi-periphery'. Colonies with economies based on slave labour formed an outer zone, or 'periphery'. The core states, with their more advanced economies, are considered to have drawn-in raw materials and resources from both the periphery and semi-periphery. At the same time they were able to sell manufactured goods to the other two zones, thus expanding their own economies. Control of the world system depended upon seapower, and there was continuous conflict for naval dominance between Spain, Holland, England and France until the eighteenth century.

* Although most historians would agree that all these suggested elements were present in some places at some times, many feel that the concept of the world system is too complex and over sophisticated. They consider that, in reality, world trade developed in a much more haphazard and accidental fashion. At the same time there is increasing scepticism about the supposed link between capitalism and protestantism. However, it is recognised that for large-scale industry to develop there had to be a long-distance trade network to distribute goods and to collect raw materials as cheaply as possible. At the same time, if greater

production was to be encouraged, there was a need to expand overseas markets. This required a range of accessible markets, and skilled mariners with enough large ships to carry out the products for sale, and to return with raw materials. Equally, the internal market had to have good communications by road, river and sea to distribute raw materials and deliver manufactures to ports for embarkation. To a large extent the Tudor economy is seen as being deficient in all these respects, and it is this that is thought to explain the many economic problems facing the Elizabethan government in 1600.

3 Overseas Trade: The Antwerp–London Funnel 1450–1550

Like the rest of Western Europe, England had suffered from the fifteenth-century trade recession. By then 'white' cloth (see page 45) had replaced wool as the country's main export. In the 1440s some 55,000 cloths a year were exported, compared with 9,000 sacks (a sack contained 240 pounds) of wool. As the recession deepened in the 1450s cloth sales fell to an annual 35,000 and wool exports went down to 8,000 sacks a year. Similarly, the sale of raw materials such as tin, lead and hides was on a reduced scale. Imports, particularly of wine, were also falling. At the same time England's diplomatic position had deteriorated. Defeat in the Hundred Years War had resulted in the loss of all English territories in France except for the port of Calais. This reverse was followed by the Wars of the Roses, a civil war lasting until the 1480s. Lacking strong government support, English merchants lost control of their markets in central Europe and the Baltic to continental rivals. By the 1460s, when trade began to recover, almost half of England's cloth exports was handled by foreigners.

    * At this stage commerce in northern and central Europe was largely controlled by regulated companies of merchants. They were organised rather like guilds, with members trading as individuals under common regulations and setting agreed prices. The company arranged convoys with fixed sailing times for mutual protection and negotiated commercial agreements with the rulers of the nations with which they traded. The companies had considerable power because they could give large loans to monarchs in return for trading privileges. The main rival to English merchants was the Hanseatic League, a powerful group of German merchants under the protection of the Holy Roman Empire. During the fifteenth century they gained great influence over English commerce and established centres, called 'steelyards', in London and other leading towns in England. Apart from the Hansards, Italian merchants, who controlled the lucrative Mediterranean trade, dealt in English cloth and brought in silk, spices and other luxuries. The major English company had been the Merchant Staplers, which had handled wool exports through its centre at Calais. However, as wool sales fell, many members had turned to supplying wool to the English rural cloth

industry. Others had joined the Merchant Adventurers, which had emerged as the major English trading company by 1500. It had been set up by wealthy members of the London livery companies to trade in cloth and mixed cargoes, and was a bitter rival of the Hanse and the Italians.

By backing Henry VII with loans, the Merchant Adventurers gained strong royal support. Through commercial treaties, such as the Magnus Intercursus of 1496, the company secured a privileged position in the Netherlands, as the main buyer of English cloth, which gave them a considerable advantage over their main competitors, the Hanse. Until the 1550s the London Merchant Adventurers dominated this trade and set up what has been called the London–Antwerp 'funnel'. During this period Antwerp was the main trading centre and money market in Western Europe. This gave London merchants all the advantages of warehousing facilities and the rudimentary bills of exchange, credit and insurance available there. Being a major entrepot (a centre for international trade), Antwerp could provide goods from all over the world almost as cheaply as they could be bought from the country of origin. This made London merchants complacent because they did not need to seek other markets. They were content to benefit from this short-distance, low-risk commerce. However, they were learning important financial skills from the Netherlanders, and began to set up similar facilities in London.

★ English cloth exports continued to expand until the 1550s. Although wool exports had fallen to a mere 4,000 sacks by the 1540s, this is taken to indicate the continued growth of the rural textile industry. By the middle of the century the annual sale of 'old draperies', especially kerseys, to the Netherlands had risen to 130,000 cloths. At the same time exports of tin, lead and hides were rising rapidly. However, this is not seen as evidence of real economic growth. England was still basically an exporter of raw materials and heavily reliant on the sale of semi-finished textiles. Moreover, the country was still dependent on imports (see the map on page 60). Although luxury goods, such as wine, spices, sugar, gems, glass, silks, playing cards, tennis balls and silverware for the elite market, were prominent, England was equally reliant upon a variety of basic necessities. Large quantities of metalwares had to bought from Germany, including cheap mass-produced armour. Saltpetre for making gunpowder, cast iron cannon from France and iron ore from Sweden were highly important. Woad, vegetable oil, salt, wax and alum, all essential in the cloth and leather industries, were supplied by Spain, France and central Europe. Timber, rope, pitch and tar for shipbuilding all came from the Baltic, and even the canvas for sails mainly came from France. In bad harvest years grain from eastern Europe had to be purchased through Danzig in the Baltic. This adverse balance of trade is seen as a clear indication of the relative technological backwardness of the early Tudor economy.

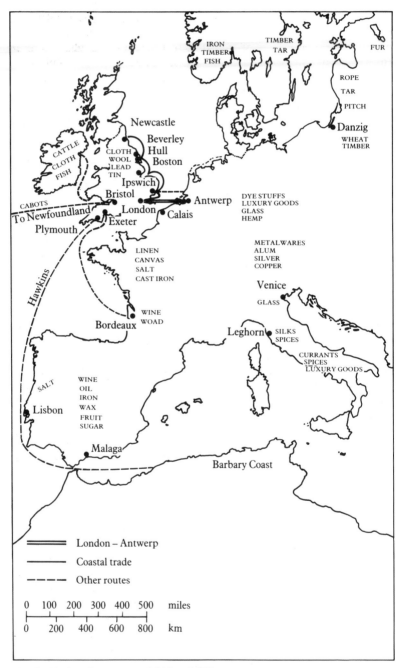

Early Tudor Commerce 1500 – 1550

At the same time it is considered that there was a serious imbalance in the distribution of trade. The London–Antwerp 'funnel' concentrated overseas commerce on London at the expense of other English ports. In the middle of the fifteenth century London had controlled half of the export of English cloth. By the 1550s 90 per cent of overseas trade went through the capital. Ports such as Bristol, Sandwich, Colchester, Boston, Hull and Beverley lost a large amount of their trade to Londoners. From the 1520s there were numerous complaints to the Privy Council from other leading towns, such as Norwich, York and Newcastle, that the Londoners were preventing them trading in the continental markets. Even the port of Southampton, which had prospered until the 1520s from the Italian luxury trade, had fallen into decay by 1550. Only a few of the outports, such as Exeter and Ipswich, maintained their cloth trade, and even then it amounted to only 5 per cent of total exports. Some historians see this as part of the 'urban crisis', with many of the outports facing serious problems during the first half of the century. Some, such as the Channel ports and Boston and Beverley, never really recovered.

The general effect of the dominance of London was to add to the prosperity of the south-east at the expense of the north and west. The growth of the London money markets is seen to have been a major factor in this situation. As Londoners became more financially skilful, merchants from all over England found it cheaper to ship their goods through the capital. A ship owner wishing to cover the cost of a voyage could borrow £100 in London for the payment of an additional £25 on its return, whereas it would cost £40 in other ports. However, this was an important development because Londoners were acquiring the expertise to finance the long-distance voyages necessary for world trade. Another beneficial consequence was that Londoners were also taking trade from foreign competitors. At the beginning of the century at least half England's overseas trade was controlled by foreign merchants, but by the 1550s 70 per cent was in English hands.

4 Other Areas of English Overseas Trade 1500–50

Another problem with England's trading position until the 1550s is considered to have been the lack of markets other than Antwerp. Apart from the ease of this trade, diplomatic considerations deterred English merchants from infringing Habsburg commercial monopolies. As early as 1497 Bristol merchants helped finance the Venetian navigator, John Cabot, in a voyage of exploration to Newfoundland, and further support was given to his son, Sebastian, to explore the area around Hudson Bay. However, although Henry VII rewarded Cabot with a fee of £10, lack of interest in the Newfoundland fisheries and fears of offending Spain meant that these expeditions were not followed up. Suggestions for the need to find alternative routes to open up Far

Eastern trade while avoiding Spanish monopolies, such as contained in Robert Thorne's *Declaration of the Indies* of 1527, were given little attention. Only a few adventurous merchants from West Country ports made voyages to the Caribbean, Africa and Brazil. In the 1520s and again in the 1540s William Hawkins of Plymouth traded along the west coast of Africa for pepper and ivory, and sailed across the Atlantic to Brazil. Although there was some interest in such voyages, opposition from the London Merchant Adventurers made it difficult to raise the finance for them.

Apart from this tentative interest in world trade, a few new markets were opened up before the 1550s. As they were shut out of the lucrative Antwerp trade, merchants from the out-ports began to look for other outlets for their goods. Along the east coast merchants from Newcastle, Hull and Ipswich were beginning to re-establish links with the Baltic, Iceland and northern Europe. In the south-west, Bristol, Poole, Plymouth and Exeter continued to trade with Spain, France and Ireland. Even so, by 1550 the great volume of trade was still concentrated on Antwerp. It was at this point that London merchants were jolted out of their complacency by events in Western Europe, and were forced to find alternative markets.

5 The Antwerp Slump and the Reorganisation of English Trade 1550–1600

By 1550 the commercial situation in Antwerp was becoming increasingly precarious. The continuous rise in cloth sales during the 1540s had, to a large extent, been artificially produced by England's severe financial problems. Debasements of the coinage (see page 24) had reduced the value of sterling against continental currencies, and so had made English cloth cheaper to buy. In 1551, as a result of the long war against France and Scotland, England was bankrupt and heavily in debt to continental bankers. William Cecil, the Secretary of State, and Sir Thomas Gresham, for the Treasury, were entrusted with the task of restoring stability. The sale of Crown assets and a large loan from the Merchant Adventurers and other London merchants averted the immediate crisis. Then Gresham was sent to the Netherlands and supplied with £12,000 a week to manipulate the money markets. He was so successful that all outstanding loans were repaid and the value of sterling was restored. This was by no means the end of the commercial problems. The growth of more radical Protestantism in the Church of England under Edward VI soured relations with the Habsburgs. The Emperor Charles began to place greater restrictions on English merchants in the Netherlands. Furthermore, the signs of increasing persecution of Protestants resulted in many Merchant Adventurers leaving Antwerp. Although relations improved under Mary I, this coincided with the beginning of the breakdown of political stability in

Western Europe (see page 55) which led to a re-orientation of English trade.

* The changed political situation on the continent was to facilitate England's entry into world trade, but this was not immediately apparent in the 1550s. Some merchants from west coast ports seized the opportunity to begin trading in the Mediterranean. William Hawkins began to sell cloth and iron in exchange for sugar and saltpetre along the Barbary coast from 1551. His example was soon followed by other shipowners, who were trading in west Africa as far south as the Gold Coast by 1553. However, until 1558 the Anglo- Habsburg alliance was still in place and London merchants were wary of infringing Spanish and Portuguese monopolies. For this reason they favoured the idea of finding an alternative route to the Far East avoiding the Spanish and Portuguese sea-routes around Cape Horn and the Cape of Good Hope. The mathematician and geographer, John Dee (see page 65), advocated a scheme to reach China via a north-eastern passage. A joint stock enterprise, the Company of Merchant Adventurers of England for the Discovery of Lands Unknown, was floated in 1553 by a consortium of privy councillors and London merchants, who each invested £25. Sebastian Cabot, who had been given a pension of £100 a year by Henry VIII in 1547 to live in England, was made the governor of the company. Under the command of Sir Hugh Willoughby and Richard Chancellor, three ships set out under orders drawn up by Cabot and with letters of introduction to the ruler of China. Two of the ships were lost off Lapland in 1554, but Chancellor succeeded in reaching the White Sea port of Archangel. Here he was able to establish diplomatic contact with Ivan IV, the ruler of Muscovy. As a result the Muscovy Company was formed in 1555 to trade with Russia. Although this provided an alternative to the Baltic as a source of timber, pitch and other ship-building materials, Russia did not offer a large market for English cloth or provide spices and other Oriental luxuries. For this reason, the north-east sea route proved impractical and the company tried to pioneer an overland route to the Far East. Anthony Jenkins, a company agent, journeyed to the Caspian Sea, finally reached Persia in 1562 and established a trade in Persian carpets in exchange for English cloth, but found the old overland 'silk route' too dangerous to use.

* This type of joint stock enterprise became increasingly popular as the century progressed because political instability abroad, and the greater cost of longer voyages, made the risk too great for individual merchants to bear. Unlike the old regulated companies, joint stock companies were floated by several hundred investors, mainly from London, who did not trade as individuals, but shared equally in the profits or losses. Some were created for a single voyage, others became permanent. Many were formed under royal charter, which gave them a monopoly of trade in a designated area and the right to negotiate with foreign powers. Such companies were favoured by the government

because they were a means of controlling overseas trade and a useful source of loans. In return the state, theoretically, provided naval protection against foreign powers and privateers and support through embargoes, tariffs and navigation acts, which only allowed goods to be carried in English ships. However, up to 1600 the government did not have the military resources to offer any effective protection to English merchants. Historians no longer consider that joint stock companies had such a great impact on late Tudor trade as was once thought. It is considered that many of the companies were under-financed and frequently created for quick profits, rather than for sound commercial reasons (see page 69).

6 The Slave Trade, Privateering and Exploration

After Elizabeth I's accession in 1558 England's deteriorating relations with the continent made the need for new enterprises very apparent. In 1564 the Merchant Adventurers were forced to leave Antwerp. Although they were given a new royal charter and tried to establish themselves in various continental towns, they found competition with the Hanseatic League very difficult. Finally they were driven from the continent altogether in 1597, and in the same year the Hansards were expelled from all their English centres. In 1563 William Cecil addressed Parliament on the need to encourage the fishing industry in order to train Englishmen in the art of seamanship. To this end both Fridays and Wednesdays were designated as fish days, on which the eating of meat was illegal. This did much to revive the off-shore fishing industry and reawaken interest in the Newfoundland cod fisheries (see page 61). At the same time, under the leadership of John Hawkins, the son of William Hawkins, work was begun in royal shipyards, such as Chatham, to improve the design of English ships so that they could compete with those of their maritime rivals. This all formed part of the 'cold war' period of relationships with Spain when England began to challenge the Spanish and Portuguese trading monopolies.

In 1562 John Hawkins organised an expedition to break into the highly lucrative slave trade begun by Spain in 1517 to supply African labour for their American plantations. He successfully acquired 300 slaves from Senegal and exchanged them in Hispaniola (Haiti) for sugar, hides and gold. His second voyage in 1564 was well subscribed, the queen and many privy councillors being stock holders. Although the Spanish officials in America were less cooperative, the expedition was still very profitable. A third voyage in 1567 proved disastrous. Hawkin's ships had to shelter from tropical storms in the Mexican port of San Juan de Ulloa, where they were attacked and mainly destroyed by a Spanish fleet. Only Hawkins and Francis Drake escaped in two ships, and all the shareholders lost their investment. Spain had temporarily restored her American monopoly, but it is considered that the English were beginning to gain valuable experience in what was later in the seventeenth century to become the very profitable 'triangular trade' based in Bristol.

Embittered by this experience, Hawkins and Drake turned from legitimate trade to piracy in the Caribbean and Spanish America. In 1572–3 they organised raids on the Isthmus of Panama to cut the Spanish treasure routes, and captured enough bullion to make considerable profits for the stockholders. However, later adventurers, such as John Oxenham, found the Spanish defences more organised and most of them were captured and executed. Nevertheless, during the 1570s many merchants and adventurers combined privateering with trade. From bases on the Scilly Islands they raided across the Atlantic to the Americas and along the African coast. The culmination of this phase of piracy, exploration and trade was Francis Drake's circumnavigation of the world in the Golden Hind between 1577 and 1580, which was financed by a court syndicate. After rounding Cape Horn he sailed up the Pacific coast of America, claimed San Francisco Bay for England and crossed the Pacific to the East Indies in 1579. Apart from plunder, mainly from the captured Spanish treasure ship the Cacafuego, Drake brought six tons of cloves back from the East Indies. In all, the cargo is estimated to have been worth £1.5 million, a profit of 4,700 per cent. Other English attempts before 1600 to round Cape Horn, apart from Sir Thomas Cavendish in 1586–8, all met with failure. Again, although no lasting successes were achieved during this phase of maritime activity, it is considered that valuable experience had been gained.

* At this time most English merchants preferred to engage in less dangerous enterprises. For this reason more attention was given to finding an alternative route to the Far East. The most successful initiative was the opening of trade with Turkey (known as the Levantine trade) in currants, spices, silks and oil, in exchange for cloth. As the volume of trade increased, the London-based Levant Company was chartered in 1579. Anxious to avoid the high prices charged by Turkish middlemen, agents of the company were sent to explore the overland routes to the East. In 1583 John Newbury and Ralph Fitch travelled to Baghdad and then on to Basra, from where they sailed to India. Fitch journeyed on to Siam and Burma, finally returning to London in 1591 with much useful information about Oriental trade. Attention also turned to finding a north-west passage to the Far East. This idea was supported by John Dee and Sir Humphrey Gilbert, who had written A Discourse of a Discovery of a New Passage to Cathai in 1566. In 1576 Gilbert financed three ships under Martin Frobisher to explore the area around Baffin Island north of Hudson Bay. They claimed success and to have found gold. The Company of Cathay was formed, but subsequent voyages met with failure and the gold proved to be worthless quartz. Another geographer, John Davis, who invented

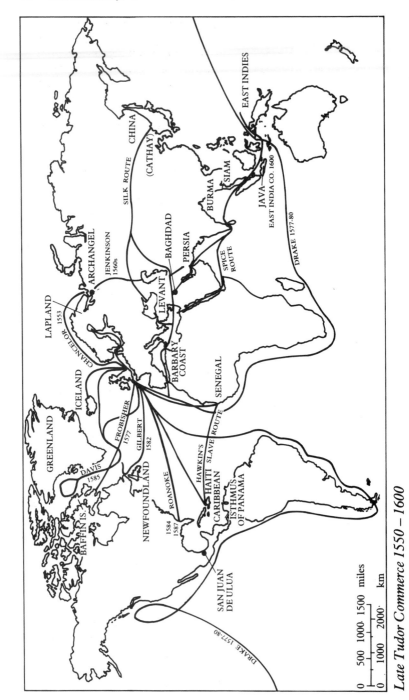

Late Tudor Commerce 1550 – 1600

a quadrant for locating latitude, was equally convinced of the existence of a north-west passage. He made three voyages to the region of Baffin Island between 1585 and 1587, but these were equally unsuccessful.

At the same time, many provincial merchants were trying to re-establish less risky trade with the continent and in the Mediterranean. Bristol merchants were beginning to establish useful outlets for cloth through the Netherlands, Calais and Cadiz. Simultaneously merchants from the south-west were building on earlier contacts along the African coast to trade cloth for gold and ivory. Along the east coast, traders from Hull and Newcastle, encouraged by the declining power of the Hanse, reopened commercial links in the Baltic, Scandinavia and Iceland. They were soon joined by London merchants, who formed the Eastland Company for Baltic trade in 1579. In many respects these developments are seen as having greater commercial significance than the more spectacular attempts to break into world trade. For much of the seventeenth century the growth of Baltic and Mediterranean markets were the mainstay of English commerce.

7 Colonisation, the Armada, Recession and Far Eastern Trade

During the 1580s worsening relations with Spain, and increasing government concern over unemployment and over-population, led to schemes for colonisation in North America. The concept of colonisation aroused considerable enthusiasm in England. One of its chief exponents was Richard Hakluyt, whose book *Principal Navigations*, published in full in 1589, is the main source of information about early English exploration. Hakluyt saw colonies as providing new markets and being the source of raw materials and bullion. He also considered that sending out colonists to America would overcome the problem of unemployment and vagrancy in England. Sir Humphrey Gilbert, undaunted by his earlier failures, proposed to establish a colony on the north-east coast of America. In 1583 he sailed with five ships and 200 colonists to St Johns in Newfoundland, which had become an international fishing port. In spite of problems, he claimed the settlement for England and sailed on with three ships to Novia Scotia. However, the ship carrying the colonists and provisions was wrecked, and Gilbert, returning to England for fresh supplies, was drowned when his ship sank.

[Hakluyt writing before the outcome of Gilbert's voyage was known]
1 Now to show how the same is likely to prove very profitable and beneficial to the whole realm. It is very clear that the greatest jewel of this realm, and the chieftest strength force . . . is the multitude of ships, masters and mariners to assist the . . . royal
5 navy of her Majesty . . . And the chieftest cause why our

Englishmen do not go so far westerly [is because] they have no
succour and safe harbour in those parts. But if our nation were
once placed here . . . they might fish as long as they pleased
themselves . . . Besides this, it will prove a general benefit unto
10 our country that through, this occasion, not only a great number
of men which do now live idly at home, and are burdensome,
chargeable and unprofitable to this realm, shall thereby be set to
work, but also children . . . And, moreover our idle women
(which this realm may well spare) shall also be employed.

Gilbert's fate did not lessen the enthusiasm for colonisation. In 1584
Sir Walter Raleigh proposed to establish a colony near modern
Virginia. This area, it was considered, would be safe from Spanish
attack and would have a suitable climate to provide many raw materials
then only obtainable from the Mediterranean. The expedition was led
by Sir Richard Grenville, who took 10 ships and 108 colonists to
Roanoke Island. Unfortunately the settlers, who were mainly Londoners, found it difficult to adapt to the conditions and quarrelled with the
coastal Indians. Some of the colonists were rescued by Drake, but the
remainder died. In 1587 a second expedition, led by John White, tried
to establish a settlement on the same site. White went back to England
for fresh supplies, but was delayed by the Armada campaign. When he
returned in 1591 the colonists had disappeared and the site was
abandoned. Four years later Raleigh led an expedition to South
America in search of El Dorado, the city of gold. Although he explored
along the Orinoco river, he found no gold, and the venture was a
financial disaster. All these expensive failures showed that colonisation
required careful planning, management, and sound financial backing.
    * The growing hostility of Spain and the decline in commercial
activity created a general feeling of pessimism on the eve of the Armada
campaign.

Lord Burghley to Sir Christopher Hatton on the State of Trade,
1587
1 This great matter of the lack of vent [sale] not only of clothes,
which presently is the greatest, out of all other English commodities which are restrained from Spain, Portugal, Barbary, France,
Flanders, Hamburg and the States [Holy Roman Empire] cannot
5 but in the process of time work a great danger and dangerous
issue to the people of the realm, who, heretofore, in time of
outward peace, lived thereby, and without it must either perish
for want, or fall into violence . . . which is the print of rebellion.

Although the defeat of the Armada in 1588 removed the danger of
invasion, and gave England command of the seas, it did not improve
the commercial situation. Many merchants and adventurers took the

opportunity to turn to privateering. In 1595 Drake and Hawkins led an expedition of 27 ships to pillage Spanish possessions in America. They found the Spaniards well prepared, many ships were lost and both Drake and Hawkins died at sea. This failure added to the general gloom of the 1590s. However, English command of the sea did encourage renewed interest in the Far Eastern trade. Attempts in 1591 and 1595 to sail to the East Indies via the Cape of Good Hope failed. When the East India Company was formed by 242 London merchants in 1600, James Lancaster, who had already sailed to the East Indies, was put in command of the first expedition. He sailed with five ships in 1601, taking £30,000 in silver, as well as iron, lead, tin and cloth, which it was hoped to trade for gems, camphor, sulphur and spices. A factory (trading warehouse) was set up in Java and a brisk exchange of goods was established. However, there was no demand for the heavy English cloth. Nevertheless, the fleet returned to England in 1603 with goods worth £3 million.

8 Summary: Overseas Trade

Although this success did bring some encouragement, historians agree with contemporaries in the pessimistic view that English overseas commerce was declining by the end of the century. In the 1560s woollen cloth is estimated to have comprised 80 per cent of all exports, but other textiles, such as linen, silk, cottons and canvas, made up 40 per cent of imports. Commodities such as oil, dyestuffs, metalwares and wine accounted for another 28 per cent of imports. Even in the 1560s imports considerably exceeded exports and this unfavourable balance of trade had worsened by 1603. The sale of heavy woollen cloth was falling, although this was partially compensated for by the export of 'new draperies' to the Levant, Africa and the Mediterranean, which had risen to 25 per cent of total exports. Most imports still came from northern Europe, with only 30 per cent from the Mediterranean and a mere 6 per cent from America and the Orient. There is general agreement that the main problem for overseas commerce, as in other areas of the economy, was a lack of financial institutions and a shortage of investment. Although the London money market was being improved, the absence of a bank along continental lines was a serious impediment to trade. Most overseas ventures had to be financed privately, or by short-term joint stock companies. Investment came mainly from London merchants, with the aristocracy and gentry contributing only about 20 per cent of overseas financing. City merchants and courtiers were more interested in quick profits from privateering than in long-term investment and planning. Government backing for such projects, and the granting of too many monopolies only made the situation worse. Even so, there was some cause for optimism. England was catching up with its competitors in learning the skills of maritime trade. During the second half of the century the English merchant marine doubled from some 50,000 tons. New, fast, 500 ton galleons, such as the Revenge, were being built, which helped to maintain English power at sea. Lessons in the art of carrying large cargoes over long distances were being learned from the capture of 1,000 ton Portuguese carracks used in the Far Eastern trade. Above all, there was an encouraging spirit of enterprise. Many of the Elizabethan initiatives were misguided, but they did lay the foundations for expansion in the next century.

9 Internal Trade: The Urban Hierarchy, Markets and Fairs

Many historians consider that developments in internal trade made a greater contribution to the economy than the more spectacular overseas enterprises. Even so, it is thought that there was little real progress before 1600, and that the overall picture was one of great continuity. The growth of the London markets is seen as the major driving force behind the increasing volume of internal trade. At the same time, developing specialisation and regionalism added to the amount of more long-distance exchanges. The Tudors were careful to regulate the urban marketing structure by calling-in and then re-issuing amended charters for markets and fairs, and by closing down unlicensed rural markets. However, private and governmental efforts in trying to improve the infrastructure of roads, rivers and coastal shipping were essential if there was to be any significant expansion in the volume of goods being moved.

* The Tudor pattern of internal trade was still based on the system of town markets and fairs created during the middle ages. The sharp fall in the late medieval population is thought to have reduced the number of towns from about 2,000 to about 700 in the sixteenth century. These ranged in size from London, with an estimated population of 200,000 by 1600, to small market centres of about 1,000 people. It is very difficult to generalise about towns because their backgrounds and histories are so different. However, urban historians have created a number of broad criteria to define early modern towns as opposed to large villages. It is considered that these were: density of population, specialist economic activities, a sophisticated social hierarchy, a recognisable governmental structure, and having a strong impact upon the surrounding countryside. Every town did not have to display all these features, and many of the smaller ones met only one or two of them. To make the position clearer, it has been suggested that early modern towns can be formed into a hierarchy. At the top was London, which was beginning to exert an increasingly national influence by 1600. Next came the five provincial capitals of Norwich, Bristol, York, Newcastle and Exeter. They were all considerably smaller than London – the largest, Norwich, having a population of only 15,000 by 1600 – but they

all had a regional influence greater than other towns. Below them came a wide range of county towns, some of which were corporate boroughs, with charters from the Crown. A number of these towns, such as Buckingham or Northampton, were single centres for a county, but in some counties there were several towns of equal status. There were considerable variations in size and function among county towns. Some, such as Hull and Yarmouth, were primarily ports and fishing centres, while others, such as Canterbury and Oxford, had major religious or educational status. Towns like Beverley and Colchester were primarily industrial, while Banbury and St Ives (in Cambridgeshire) had specialist markets or fairs. At the bottom were many market or small country towns, scarcely distinguishable from villages, which served as marketing centres for the hundred (a subdivision of a county) in which they were situated. The common feature of all towns was that they provided the markets through which internal trade was carried out.

* Increasing specialisation made London and the regions more dependent upon goods being carried over longer distances. For this purpose the town markets relied on the network of roads and rivers linking them together and upon coastal shipping carrying bulky goods, such as coal, grain and metal ores. In this respect, London and the provincial capitals all had good communications. London was the centre of the old Roman and medieval road system, and had good water access via the sea and the river Thames. The provincial capitals all had good sea approaches, Norwich and York through the outports of Yarmouth and Hull, and stood on major river systems which linked them with their hinterlands. To a greater or lesser extent good transport facilities were essential for all towns, and even many inland towns were able to function as river ports. Rapid demographic growth and regional specialisation during the sixteenth century expanded market demand, and increased the volume of goods that had to be moved. The government, local landowners and town authorities all made attempts to improve the quality of communications, especially after the 1580s. Government support for the fishing industry and shipbuilding enhanced coastal trade, particularly along the east coast between Newcastle and London. Local commissions and committees all over the country worked to improve roads and make rivers more navigable. Special attention was paid to the Thames because of the needs of the London food markets. Success was limited, and the only new stretch to be made navigable by 1600 was between Henley and Abingdon in Oxfordshire. As with most areas of the economy, historians consider that the major improvement to the communications infrastructure only came in the next century. Even so, it is thought that there was a significant increase in the numbers of carriers operating river barges, and that the more efficient carts and waggons were beginning to replace pack animals on the roads.

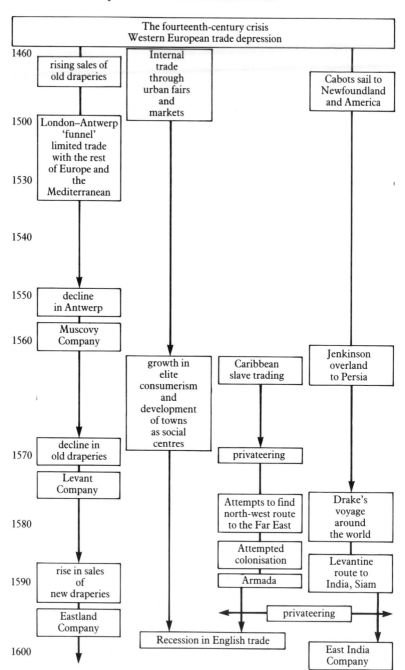

The fourteenth-century crisis
Western European trade depression

1460 — rising sales of old draperies

Internal trade through urban fairs and markets

Cabots sail to Newfoundland and America

1500 — London–Antwerp 'funnel' limited trade with the rest of Europe and the Mediterranean

1530

1540

1550 — decline in Antwerp

Muscovy Company

1560

growth in elite consumerism and development of towns as social centres

Caribbean slave trading

Jenkinson overland to Persia

1570 — decline in old draperies

Levant Company

privateering

1580

Attempts to find north-west route to the Far East

Drake's voyage around the world

Attempted colonisation

Armada

Levantine route to India, Siam

1590 — rise in sales of new draperies

Eastland Company

privateering

1600

Recession in English trade

East India Company

Summary – The Economy: Trade and Commerce

10 Summary: The Tudor Economy

Most historians share this gloomy picture of the Tudor economy by the end of the century. England was still dependent on textiles as the only major export. As yet insufficient markets had been established to sell the 'new draperies' to compensate for the loss of employment caused by the decline of the 'old draperies'. It is true that there had been technological improvements in agriculture, industry and commerce. However, these are seen as bringing England more into a position to compete with her continental rivals in the next century, rather than as creating immediate economic growth. Moreover, production levels were low and expansion was hampered by the lack of banks and other financial institutions. In any case there was a lack of investment, with the aristocracy and gentry being more interested in putting money into land and houses than into the economy. At the same time demand was sparse. Although there was increased elite consumption, self-sufficiency, unemployment and poverty kept purchasing among the lower orders to a minimum. However, the picture is regarded as not being totally pessimistic. The potential economic crisis of the 1550s had been averted. Furthermore, although the economy appeared to be stagnating in the 1590s, improvements in the infrastructure, agriculture, industry and commerce were to create economic growth by the 1660s.

Making notes on 'The Economy: Overseas and Internal Trade'

Section 1 examines some of the difficulties of quantitatively assessing the levels of external and internal trade and outlines the major shift in the direction of Tudor overseas trade. Section 2 discusses some of the main theories explaining this expansion and you need to make careful notes so that you understand the various interpretations. The development of overseas trade falls into two distinct parts. Section 3 examines the period from 1450 to 1550 when English commerce was dominated by the export of cloth via the London–Antwerp 'funnel'. You need to think carefully about the good and the bad effects that this had on the economy, and the extent to which England had become dependent on imported goods. Other areas of English trade in the first half of the sixteenth century are discussed in section 4 and you should consider why these were so limited. After the 1550s the trading pattern changed. Section 5 examines how English traders tried to develop new markets and trading techniques and you need to think carefully about whether these strategies were successful. Sections 6 and 7 look at the ways in which some of these new strategies were put in effect. You must consider the respective importance (and the associated problems) of the

Mediterranean trade, contacts with the Far East and colonisation before deciding what were the most significant developments by 1600. At the same time, you need to remember the importance of internal trade. Section 9 examines the urban hierarchy and the types of trading associated with it. You should make careful notes of the whole section, and consider the problems that limited the growth of the internal markets. You need to consider the reasons for this, and whether the problem was caused by the severely limited purchasing power of the lower orders. Refer back to your notes on chapter 3 to consider the overall state of the economy in 1600.

Answering essay questions on 'The Economy: Overseas and Internal Trade'

England's overseas trade – especially its changing pattern and the reasons for it – during the sixteenth century is a natural choice of topic for examiners to make, if only because historians have disagreed so much about it. Such a topic lends itself readily to the setting of 'challenging statement' questions. Examine the following examples:

1. How far would you agree with the opinion that 'English seamen contributed greatly to England's wealth and prestige in the second half of the sixteenth century'?
2. 'The pattern of English trade changed significantly in the second half of the sixteenth century, but not through choice.' Discuss.
3. 'The Elizabethan age witnessed a considerable expansion of England's overseas trade.' How valid is this assessment?
4. 'English colonial development in the late sixteenth century was largely the result of the need to find new markets.' Discuss this view.

If you carry out the normal first two tasks in preparing to answer 'challenging statement' questions (identifying the component parts of the quotation and identifying what the examiner is asking you to do) you will find that question 4 is by far the most straightforward. It is an example of the simplest type of 'challenging statement' question in which there is a single issue (what were the causes of English colonial development in the late sixteenth century?) and a single explanation suggested (the need to find new markets). You are asked to discuss the 'completeness' of this explanation and to assess the relative importance of other possible explanations. What other causes of English colonial development would you need to discuss in your essay?

The other three questions are more complex but should offer no particular difficulties once the normal first two tasks have been carried out on them. Carrying out these tasks on the three questions would show you how well prepared you are to tackle 'challenging statement' questions in examination conditions.

Sometimes seemingly very straightforward questions are set on this topic; by now you should be used to identifying the snags before you begin to answer them. The following examples share the same potential snags:

5. Explain how and why English export markets changed between 1550 and 1650.
6. What were the reasons for, and the results of, overseas exploration and trading enterprise between 1558 and 1603?
7. How far and for what reasons did English merchants change their products and markets between 1485 and 1603?

What are the snags? Clues are to be found in the following statements – i) examiners are likely to penalise answers to question 5 which show no knowledge of the period after 1603, and ii) few answers to these questions are likely to be awarded more than 50–60 per cent of the available marks. If you are to do well by answering easy questions, especially good essay-planning techniques are necessary! So, one of the most dangerous traps you can fall into is beginning to write your answer to a 'simple' question without spending a few minutes planning it.

Source-based questions on 'The Economy: Overseas and Internal Trade'

1 The Importance of Overseas Trade
Carefully read the extracts from Hakluyt and Burghley given on pages 67 and 68. Answer the following questions.
a) What did Hakluyt argue would be the direct advantages of establishing an English colony in America? Read the next question before answering this. (*4 marks*)
b) What are the indirect advantages referred to in the last two sentences (beginning 'Besides this') of the first extract? (*3 marks*)
c) What particularly worried Burghley about the decline in the cloth trade? (*3 marks*)
d) What assumptions did the two writers share about the poor? Explain your answer by referring to the extracts. (*5 marks*)
e) How far were Hakluyt's hopes and Burghley's fears realised by 1603? (*5 marks*)

CHAPTER 5

Society: The Landed and Urban Elites

1 Introduction

The sixteenth century is seen by all historians as a period when there was a significant shift in social relationships at all levels. To understand the nature of social change it is necessary to consider society as a whole. The structure of Tudor society depended upon the relationship between its component parts. Contemporaries saw their own society in terms of a series of checks and balances which maintained social harmony. The next four chapters examine changes in attitude and outlook which helped to promote social development in England during the period. However, any such changes must be seen as being long term. The major feature of Tudor society was of underlying continuity.

* In terms of general social theories, the sixteenth century is seen as forming only part of a continuous process which began in the fourteenth century and ended with the industrial society of the nineteenth century. Just as historians disagree as to what happened in the 'fourteenth-century crisis' (see page 5), there is no agreement as to what was happening in the sixteenth century. Marxist historians maintain that social changes were mainly the consequence of shifts in economic relations at all levels. Revisionist historians, on the other hand, consider that shifts of political relationships among the elites were the major influence on the social structure. Equally, other historians stress the importance of religion, culture, demography and urbanisation in the process of change. However, whatever theory is advanced, it is recognised that any explanation has to be multi-causal.

* There is considerable disagreement among Marxist historians over the explanation of what they see as the emergence of an increasingly capitalistic society in Tudor England. The most orthodox theory is that there was a complete change in agricultural relationships (see page 34). As a result of the changes in the fourteenth century it is considered that the peasantry had been strong enough to free themselves from many of the feudal labour and other services during the fifteenth century. This gave them much greater control over their smallholdings at the expense of the landed elites. However, it is thought that under the Tudors the nobility and gentry used their political power to push up rent levels. At the same time some landlords, ignoring government legislation (see page 39), enclosed their estates. Many peasant families were unable to pay the higher rents, or lost their livelihood through enclosure, and had

to give up their smallholdings. This meant that they had to work for wages in farming or rural industry, or in a town. It is this increase in the number of those dependent upon wages that is seen as creating a new social and economic relationship. There was a widening gap between the landowner, industrialist and self-employed craftsman, and the landless, propertyless wage earner. Some Marxist historians see this polarisation as the cause of greater popular discontent, which they consider to mark the growth of class conflict.

Other Marxist historians offer alternative explanations for the emergence of a capitalistic society. It has been suggested that the growth of world trade (see page 56) made labour relationships based on wages and market forces more attractive than the old feudal ones to both landlords and peasants. Estate owners found it more profitable to produce food for sale and to work their land by wage labour. Some peasant smallholders used the situation either to acquire more land to become yeomen selling food for the market, or to give up their land altogether and to work for wages. Many preferred to retain their smallholdings and remained independent. This is seen as creating conflict between market forces and self-sufficiency. Some Marxist historians attach more importance to the spread of urban and industrial relationships, already based on wages, into the countryside. They see this as the essential step towards a capitalistic society. Successful merchants, lawyers and industrialists bought country estates which they ran along commercial lines. These methods were adopted by their neighbours, and so began to change the attitudes of rural society. This is seen as creating a new class, the bourgeoisie, consisting of the gentry, yeomen, merchants, industrialists and self-employed craftsmen. The Crown is considered to have favoured this group because it could use its members to staff the growing state civil service and so reduce the influence of the nobility. This, it is thought, created class conflict between the bourgeoisie and the nobility.

* Revisionist historians, while agreeing that this process of social change began with the feudal crisis, offer an entirely different explanation. For them, social restructuring resulted from shifts in political relations among the elites caused by the rise of the state. The feudal anarchy of the late middle ages (see page 7) had enabled the Tudors to gain authority at the expense of the nobility. This meant that the state was able to centralise political power and reduce the influence of the nobility in the provinces. This is seen as making the nobility, and the other landed elites, dependent upon the Crown for support. To maintain their social, political and economic position they had to rely upon royal patronage to give offices at court, in the government or in military service. This created rivalry among the landed elites, and with the rising commercial and professional groups from the towns for royal favour. Revisionist historians do not see the rise of capitalism or changes among the lower orders as being significant.

* Many historians consider that these interpretations over-simplify the situation. Some see the Renaissance and the Reformation as being particularly important in promoting social change. It is felt that both helped to break down the power of the Church and to reduce the influence of the clergy. In this way the old medieval sacerdotal society, based on the values of the Church, was replaced by one which was more secular and individualistic. Even by the end of the fifteenth century, the Renaissance is considered to have been encouraging literacy among the landed and urban elites (see page 137). This is seen as breaking down the clergy's monopoly on education, and reducing their influence in politics and the administration. This process was carried further by the English Reformation between 1530 and 1570. The 'protestant work ethic' is seen as emphasising the individualism, commercialism and competition which created a new bourgeois outlook. It is suggested that many of the elites adopted moderate protestantism so that they could benefit from market forces.

Many historians agree with C. Hill that the medieval Church was 'the dead hand' holding back trade and inhibiting competition. At the same time the seizure and sale of monastic property by the Crown is thought to have promoted social mobility by making land available to new entrants, such as lawyers, merchants and industrialists, into the landed elites. Equally it is argued that the spoliation of the Church helped the nobility to recover from their economic problems following the 'fourteenth-century crisis'. By emphasising the importance of education, and attacking traditional customs and rituals, protestantism is seen as undermining popular culture and with it the old fabric of society (see page 125). New rational relationships, based on legal rights, time and money, began to replace the feudal values of elite hospitality and support for the weak and the poor. This is seen as central to the break-down of the leisurely, seasonal life of the peasantry. New, disciplined relations between the elites and the lower orders were being created, based on thrift, abstinence and hard work (see page 100). This was a relationship under which unemployment and poverty were regarded as sinful idleness. It is felt that the elites began to consider it their duty to manage the lives of the lower orders so as to ensure that they were usefully employed (see page 119).

* Many social and economic historians are not convinced by any of these general theories of social change. They consider that demographic variations, and the consequent inflation or deflation, were the major influences on the social structure. The economic problems of the larger landowners were caused by the deflationary period following the Black Death of 1349, which also created a period of peasant prosperity. When the population began to recover during the sixteenth century, the situation was reversed. Landowners, industrialists and craftsmen began to benefit from the increased prices caused by inflation. At the same time rents rose because more people were looking for land. Many

smallholders were forced off the land because they could not afford the higher rents. As more people were available for work, wages did not increase as quickly as prices. Consequently the standard of living of the lower orders fell, while many of the elites were becoming wealthier. This created increased polarisation, with an ever widening gap between rich and poor (see page 105).

* All these theories suggest that Tudor society was becoming more divided. The lower orders were not just growing poorer, but were also being made increasingly remote from the elites by new commercial and cultural attitudes. Elite society is seen as becoming more varied. The old feudal nobility and gentry were being joined by entrants from agriculture, commerce, industry and rising professions, such as the law. At the same time the power of the Church appears to be in decline, and the clergy to be losing their influence in an increasingly secular society.

2 Social Models

Theories, although useful, do not in themselves make it possible to see what was actually happening during a period of very complicated social change. Equally, contemporaries found it just as difficult to assess developments within society. For this reason modern historians and contemporaries created social models to provide 'patterns' to aid their understanding. These models are simplified pictures of a society at a particular time, and they show the often small but continuous changes taking place. Models have to be used with caution because they frequently represent the ideas of a particular individual. At best they give an imaginary view of society, which may, or may not, represent reality.

* Historians see the main model of late medieval feudal society as being a pyramid of status based upon the ownership of land. At the top was the king, who was the major land owner. Below him were the dukes, earls and barons who held the great estates. They consisted of about 60 families which formed the top rank of society. Descendants of the younger sons of the nobility, and new entrants from the professions and trade, formed a second tier of smaller landowners. At the bottom of elite society were the yeomen, who had to own land at least to the value of 40 shillings a year. This landed elite is thought to have comprised about 2 per cent of the population. The base of the pyramid, representing over 90 per cent of society, was the peasantry. The 5 per cent of people, the clergy and town dwellers, outside rural society are represented as two smaller pyramids of status. Clerical status depended upon an individual's position within the Church hierarchy. In England the Archbishops of Canterbury and York, with the more important abbots, were at the top. The parish clergy and the large number of people in minor orders (those holding minor ecclesiatistical office below

a priest, such as an acolyte or an exorcist) formed the base. In the towns status depended on wealth and the holding of property. Rich merchants, master craftsmen, lawyers and other members of the professions formed a top rank above the smaller craftsmen and traders. At the bottom came the journeymen, apprentices, servants and labourers who made up the bulk of urban society. Clergy and townspeople, because they were outside the main body of feudal, agricultural society, are regarded as 'random' groups. They provided the means of movement in an otherwise stable social structure. There was social mobility within and between the hierarchies, but it was mainly among the upper levels of the three groups. Until feudalism had begun to disappear, the peasantry – by far the largest section of society – were regarded as unfree serfs. As such they were the property of their owner and forbidden by law to move or to change their social status.

* Contemporary views of late medieval society present a somewhat different picture. Feudal society was made up of three estates. Not surprisingly, in what was conceived of as a divinely ordained structure, the clergy formed the first estate. They were the direct link between God and man, and were responsible for preparing the laity for the next world and praying for the souls of the dead. The second estate consisted of the king and the greater and lesser nobility. Their duty was to rule the country and to provide military protection. The peasantry formed the third estate. Although they could be called upon for military duty in time of war, their main task was to work the land so as to provide food and other essentials for the other two estates. Lay society was bonded together by mutual obligations. The king and the nobility were held together by well-defined duties of service to each other. Similarly, the peasantry performed labour and other services for the lord of the manor on which they lived. They produced the food on which the other two estates lived and, theoretically, received military and spiritual protection in return. The stability of the social structure was maintained by the Church's concept of the 'great chain of being'. This was an imaginary line stretching from God in the heavens down to the devil at the centre of the earth. Along this line the orders of creation were arranged in their correct hierarchies. Individuals were seen to have been born into their divinely ordained place within society. Failure to carry out the duties of this social status, or any attempt to change position in society, was seen as sinful. Although this ideal was upheld by the Church it did not prevent a certain amount of social mobility, which was steadily increasing by the fourteenth century.

* The pace of social movement is thought to have quickened after 1350. Historians find it difficult to construct a model which accurately portrays the impact of this greater fluidity on Tudor society. The emergence of the gentry and the growing number of people moving into the middling groups of society are seen to be major features of the new situation. Although the number of nobles remained virtually the same,

there was a considerable increase in the number of lesser landowners immediately below them. This 'rise of the gentry' (see page 95) is thought to have been highly significant, but has caused great debate amongst historians. The growth of the middle orders of society has created equal controversy. Previously labelled as 'the rise of the middle class', this development is now commonly described as the emergence of the 'bourgeoisie' (see page 77). Such an expansion is seen to have been caused by the growth in the number of landless younger sons of the gentry and yeomen and an increase in the total of successful merchants, lawyers and administrators. It is thought that, even with the sale of monastic estates, there was insufficient land to meet demand by 1600. This meant that there was a growth in the number of people in society who had wealth but no land. The influence of the Renaissance and Reformation is seen as producing a more secular society. For this reason the clergy are considered to have lost their pre-eminent position and to have become part of the middling social group. At the same time, it is considered that the virtual disappearance of serfdom created greater diversity and geographical (although not social) mobility among the lower orders (see page 102).

L. Stone has suggested that all social groups merged into a new hierarchy of status that took the shape of a stepped pyramid. The lower orders formed the broad base. Next came the middling groups, followed by the gentry and finally the nobility. The monarch remained as the apex of society. Another proposal is for what has become known as the 'united nations building' model. This takes the form of a broad base, or podium, containing some 90 per cent of the population, among which there is considerable horizontal and geographical movement but little upward mobility. The podium has a skyscraper tower standing on it which contains the landed elites. Within the tower are lifts which are constantly coming down full of younger sons and going up half empty. Around the towers are ramps up which successful lawyers and merchants climb to join the landed elites.

* Contemporaries found it equally difficult to decide how increased mobility was influencing the structure of society. This was particularly true after the 1550s when changes were becoming more pronounced. Sir Thomas Smith, writing *The Commonwealth of England* in the 1560s, speaks of society being divided into four 'sorts': gentlemen, citizens, yeomen artificers and labourers. He then goes on to break down these categories in more detail. The first rank of gentlemen was the nobility, which contained the king, dukes, marquesses, earls, viscounts and barons. They were followed by lesser landowners, knights, esquires and gentlemen. The second general category consisted of citizens, burgesses and yeomen. Smith considered these to be important because they all held some form of office, and so had authority over others. Citizens and burgesses were those who were members of governing councils in towns, served as members of parliament or held some other

civic office. Yeomen are characterised by owning land worth 40 shillings a year, being employers and having local responsibilities. The 'fourth sort of men' were not just labourers and servants but included merchants, craftsmen and smaller husbandmen. This suggests that, for Smith, social status did not depend on wealth, but upon holding office and serving the state. Indeed, in another chapter of the book he stated clearly that 'the division of those which be participant of the common wealth is one way of them that bear office, the other of them that bear none'. It is equally clear that he upheld the patriarchal view of society. Women are seen as having no importance – 'we do reject women, as those whom nature has made to keep home and to nourish their family and children, and not to meddle with matters abroad, nor to bear office in city or common wealth no more than children and infants'. The only exception were heiresses to the crown, a duchy or an earldom, and even then it is suggested that they should be married or accept the wise advice of men.

Other Elizabethan writers seem to support such a model of society. William Harrison, a country parson, in his *Description of England* published in 1577, also divided society into the four ranks suggested by Smith. Sir Henry Unton, a Berkshire landowner, noted in his papers in the 1590s that there were four orders in society and that those holding positions of authority gained status. Writing at about the same time, John Hooker from Devon said that in the county there were four degrees of people: noblemen and gentlemen, the merchant, the yeoman and the labourer. He attributed the position of merchants in society to their wealth and describes yeomen as freeholders, farmers and husbandmen. His fourth degree consisted of all craftsmen and labourers, whether in town or countryside. In 1600 Thomas Wilson, a minor courtier and official, wrote *The State of England* in which he gave a detailed description of late Tudor society. Wilson claimed to base his social analysis on his familiarity with official records. He divided the nobility into greater and lesser groups. The greater nobility consisted of 51 lay peers, made up of 1 marquess, 19 earls, 2 viscounts and 39 barons, who together had an annual income of £220,000 from rents. Bishops are also included in this category. Their combined income was estimated at only £22,500 a year, and Wilson commented on their economic and political decline, saying that 'their wings are well clipped of late'. Among the lesser nobility he not only included knights and esquires and gentlemen, but also lawyers, professors, ministers, archdeacons and vicars. Wilson estimated that there were 500 knights, with an average income of about £1,500 a year, and 16,000 esquires having on average an income of £750 a year. Of younger sons and gentlemen he considered them too numerous to estimate. Of the remainder of this group he spoke only of the rapid growth in numbers and wealth of lawyers. He thought there were some 4,000 lawyers, the richest of whom were worth some £30,000 a year. Below the nobility came the merchants and urban elites. Some London merchants were estimated to be worth £100,000, and a Londoner owning less than £50,000 was not considered to be rich. In provincial towns, such as Norwich, a merchant with £20,000 was very wealthy. Although Wilson thought that the old yeomanry had decayed, he calculated that there were some 10,000 substantial yeomen with annual incomes in excess of £1,000, and 80,000 with incomes below £500 a year. He showed little interest in the lower orders, merely commenting that there were copyholders and cottagers, some of whom were poor and worked for low wages.

In many respects these contemporary models raise more questions than provide answers. However, certain points are made clear. All these writers are agreed that Tudor society was divided into four degrees of people. Although they are expressing individual opinions, they do appear to reflect the contemporary elite view of society. This suggests that it was generally accepted that the medieval concept of three orders had been superseded. It is apparent that society had become more secular through the influence of the Renaissance and the Reformation. The monarch and the peerage are clearly the first social rank, and the position of the clergy had declined. Their place appears to have been taken by new professional groups, particularly lawyers. There seems to be ample evidence of the rise in numbers and influence of both the gentry and yeomen. At the same time greater importance seems to have been given to the urban elites. On the other hand there is much less clarity as to where and why the various groups should be placed in the social hierarchy. There appears to have been considerable disagreement about whether social status depended on birth, land ownership, wealth, authority and office, leisure and lifestyle or education. As Smith put it, only the king can make nobles and knights, but anyone who goes to university and studies the law can live idly without manual labour, behave like a gentleman and 'shall be called master'. However, Hooker considered that gentlemen were 'all such who by birth are descended of ancient and noble parents'. While Wilson placed lawyers among the gentry, Smith put merchants without land among the lower orders.

* Such confusion seems to suggest that there was considerable social movement, certainly within the upper ranks of society, by 1600. This does not mean that the government and elites did not have a clear picture of the shape which society should take. Even after the Reformation the Tudors retained the concept of the 'great chain of being' as a means of social control which was designed to maintain the social structure and to keep the lower orders in their place. It was symbolically portrayed as the 'tree of the commonwealth', depicting a society rising from its peasant roots up to the monarch at the apex. Another political representation of society was the family. The commonwealth was seen as a family, with the monarch as the father. As children obey their father, so all citizens were expected to obey the

monarch, who, in return, protected and cared for them. The whole of society was made up of families. Social harmony and stability depended on the ability of the father to maintain order within his household by controlling his wife, children and servants. This, it was thought, would ensure that social inferiors would continue to show deference to their superiors. At the same time it maintained the patriarchal view of society, with women being strictly subordinated to men (see page 127).

    * Tudor governments tried to bolster these ideals of society by the use of the sumptuary laws. These laws had first been introduced in 1337 and were retained until 1604. The objective of this type of legislation was to control the dress and behaviour of each group within the hierarchy. Generally only the royal family could wear cloth of gold. Velvet was restricted to the nobility, and silk to the gentry. The lower orders were expected to wear sombre woollen homespuns. As the century progressed the legislation became increasingly complicated. In 1533 it was ordered that only the royal family could wear purple silk, and that scarlet and blue velvet was restricted to peers. Thereafter restrictions were set on the size of ruffs and length of cloaks, as well as where specific types and colours of cloth could be worn. Heads of households were instructed to set a good example to their children and servants. In contrast to the four acts passed before 1500, the Tudors introduced five acts and 19 proclamations (royal decrees modifying existing legislation) to enforce the sumptuary laws. This seems to indicate that population growth and inflation were increasing the amount of social mobility. Despite threatened fines and confiscation of illegal clothing, the legislation was very difficult to enforce with no effective police force. By the 1580s moralists were complaining that 'those which are neither of the nobility, gentility nor yeomanry, no, not yet any magistrate . . . go daily in silks, velvets, satins, damasks, taffetas and such like'. The proclamation of 1597 admitted that despite all previous efforts there had been no 'reformation' in the wearing of apparel. Obviously legislation designed to ensure that people wore the dress appropriate to their station in life, and so prevent social emulation, was not working. Historians see this as a clear indication of the social diversity and changing living standards present in late Tudor England.

3   Elite Social Mobility 1350–1560

There is considerable agreement that there was a change in the amount and nature of social mobility among the elites during this period. Slow but significant variations took place up to 1560, which were followed by a period of faster development lasting until 1640. However, it must be remembered that this transition was very uneven and that there was great diversity. Social mobility was more pronounced in and around towns, especially London. There was considerable continuity in the countryside, particularly in the areas away from the south-east. England can be seen as a federation of county communities, each one of which was different from its neighbour. Local culture, customs and loyalties remained very strong among the elites. Recent research has confirmed that the pattern of social development varied in almost every county. It is not thought that the influence of London (see page 150), or attempts at national centralisation from the capital, had had much impact on most county communities by 1560.

* The period from 1350 to 1500 is seen as a time when significant social and cultural changes were taking place. Concepts of the divinely ordained three estates were being replaced by a more secular outlook. Apart from the consequences of the 'fourteenth-century crisis', it is considered that the growth of literacy and the spreading use of vernacular English undermined the clergy. English was increasingly being used in official documents, the law and literature so that clerical Latin was no longer so important. At the same time technological advances in warfare, such as the use of gunpowder, reduced the effectiveness of the old military order and began to make the castle obsolete. One effect of this was to begin to change elite lifestyles and concepts of comfort (see page 136). Equally, it is thought to have begun to alter attitudes towards social status. The Statute of Additions in 1413 ordered that for official and legal purposes individuals had to be identified by name, locality, estate, degree or occupation. Social position began to be expressed in terms of wealth and the hierarchy of status became more complicated. In the Sumptuary Law of 1463 the nobility was separated from the gentry, with the lower limit of wealth for barons being set at £800 a year. Distinction was made between great knights with an income of £200, and lesser knights with only £60. The 1,200 esquires were rated at £25 a year, and the 5,000 gentlemen at £7. The Lord Mayor of London and leading lawyers were given the same status as knights and wealthy merchants were equated with esquires. This is seen as reflecting the fact that the spread of secular education was enhancing the importance of the non-clerical professions, particularly lawyers, and government officials. However it is not suggested that this had a marked effect on the elite social structure before 1560. The ownership of land remained of prime importance.

* The mechanisms of social mobility are thought to have remained much the same as they had been previously, with the ownership of land being the main objective. The king was still the principal means of social advancement. Only the Crown could create nobles and knights. However, although knighthood was theoretically a mark of military distinction, it was increasingly recognised as an honour available to those owning land worth £100 a year. Land still changed hands largely through inheritance, marriage or regrant by the Crown. It was rarely available for sale. The main reason for this was that landowners were more interested in consolidating their estates and were unwilling to

dispose of what was regarded as family land. Sales were generally limited to friends, or to further political and business alliances. As inheritance was through primogeniture, only the eldest son could succeed to the family estates. This meant that it could be difficult for younger sons and daughters to maintain their social status. Marriage was seen as a major means of improving, or retaining, social status both for an individual and the family. Daughters were regarded as highly important in the marriage market by the landed and urban elites. Essential social, political and business alliances could be cemented by marriage, or family fortunes recouped through the heiress of a wealthy merchant. It was the aim of every family to improve and safeguard its social position. This meant that the nobility married within their own ranks, and if possible into the royal family. The gentry and urban elites generally married into their county or town elites, or families from neighbouring counties. Alliances between the nobility were so important that they had to be approved by the king, and marriages among their children were frequently arranged while they were still infants. However, child marriages could be dangerous because high mortality rates meant that one of the parties might die before the marriage was consummated. This could be very expensive because marriage contracts were costly to both families. To secure a good marriage the bride's father had to pay a large dowry, usually in the form of land, to the bridegroom's family. Although legally the dowry had to be returned if death prevented the consummation, costly, long delays and even litigation might well result from such a break-down in the marriage arrangements. In addition, both families had to settle more land on the couple as a jointure, which might well be difficult to retrieve should either of them die. Furthermore, to gain the right to marry a royal ward – an orphaned heir or heiress under the guardianship of the Crown – might well cost an additional £2,000 to £3,000. For these reasons gentry parents generally preferred to wait until their children came of age (girls at 14 and boys at 16) so as to avoid the cost of rearranging marriage settlements. After marriage a woman's possessions became the property of her husband, and her duty was to produce a male heir, to manage the household and to look after the children. In an age of high mortality, second marriages were common and were used to secure social alliances. A widow was entitled to one-third of family property during her lifetime and frequently had control of all the property if the children were under-age or the marriage was childless. This made them a valuable means of social advancement. In towns it was common for apprentices, or journeymen, to marry their master's widow and so take over the business.

Apart from marriage there were various careers open to younger sons. Among the landed elites they were frequently sent to the household of a patron or relative to be trained in the military arts and the code of chivalry. Advancement through war remained an important means of social mobility. A successful military campaign could bring wealth from ransoms and booty, or the renown and patronage to start a successful career. Until the Reformation the Church offered a valuable means of upward mobility. Some younger sons who went to university went on to study theology to further an ecclesiastical career. This could enable them to become bishops, archbishops or even cardinals in the secular Church or abbots in the monastic orders in both England and on the continent. Furthermore, those who reached high ecclesiastical office because of their superior education often became members of the privy council or held other important governmental positions. On a lesser scale, daughters, by entering one of the orders of nuns, gained the opportunity of education and an alternative career to marriage. However, by the early sixteenth century the growth in secular education (see page 137) encouraged many more families to send their sons to be trained in law at the Inns of Court in London. This meant that an increasing number of government officials were recruited from this background, rather than from the Church. However, the backing of a powerful patron (see page 88), preferably at court, was essential for success in such advancement. Younger sons without such support were usually condemned to the fringes of elite society, and many plunged down into the lower orders. At the same time, because of the growth in commercialisation, more of the landed elites were beginning to apprentice their younger sons into trade.

  * These same routes of upward mobility were open to the urban and minor rural elites, but the chances of success were much less. With family land and property passing to the eldest son, the problem of providing for daughters and younger sons was just as acute as it was for the nobility and gentry. The evidence suggests that the professional groups, urban elites, yeomen, prosperous husbandmen, clothiers and industrialists were increasingly sending their sons to the universities and the Inns of Court. A career in the Church remained attractive even after the Reformation. Many more younger sons (and daughters) were apprenticed into trade from these groups than from the major landed elites. However, wealth and position were not enough to secure permanent social status for their descendants. Gentility could be acquired only through marriage, patronage or the purchase of land. Only in London were some merchant families in the city council sufficiently affluent and influential to be content to remain landless. A rapid upward route was to gain royal favour. The wealthy Pole family of Hull merchants raised loans to help Edward III to finance his wars in France, and by the beginning of the sixteenth century their descendants had risen to become Earls of Suffolk. Cardinal Wolsey, the son of an Ipswich butcher, was a notable example of the success obtainable through a clerical career. His successor, Thomas Cromwell, rose to eminence via his legal training. However, although upward mobility through royal favour could be rapid, it could equally quickly end in

disfavour or execution. This was the fate of the Poles, Wolsey and Cromwell.

Patronage at a lower level was a slower, but potentially safer, means of improving social status or gaining employment. Among the elites it was highly important to keep agents at court and in the other households so as to gain inside information. At the same time it was necessary to give gifts to encourage patronage, or as bribes.

Ysabeau du Bies to Lady Lisle, 1536 [Lord Lisle was governor of Calais]

1 Madame, I humbly recommend me to your good grace. Madame, lord the Seneschal hath on his return made me a present of a little monkey, that knoweth all manner of pretty tricks. I send it to you by this present bearer, praying you, Madame, to accept this poor
5 gift in good part. It grieveth me that it is not more worthy of the regard I have for you. My said lord, and my lady Seneschal, and Monsieur de Vervins have charged me to recommend them to your good grace, beseeching you, Madame, in conclusion, to command me to what is your good pleasure that I may obey and
10 do you service therein.

Thomas Warley to Lady Lisle, 1534

1 Right honourable and my most good lady, my duty evermore remembered . . . pleaseth it your ladyship to understand that here is a priest, a very honest man, which would gladly do service to my lord and your ladyship. And these properties he hath: he
5 writes a very fair secretary hand and text hand and Roman, and singeth surely, and playesth very cunningly [skilfully] on the organs; and he is cunning in drawing of knots in gardens [a garden designed to look like a piece of embroidery] and well seen [skilled] in grafting and keeping of cucumbers and other herbs. I
10 judge him very meet [suitable] for to do my lord and lady service.

All families were equally busy trying to advance the careers of their children, relatives or lesser members of their household. Granting patronage of this sort was another way of placing an individual under the obligation to give a favour in return. For the younger sons of the lesser, landless elites this was just the type of opening needed to start their career. Many spent their whole lives in similar types of minor office at court, or in the households of the landed elites and higher clergy.

Apart from through marriage, it was very difficult for the landless elites to obtain the land needed to give them permanent status. As it has been suggested, until the 1550s the nobility and the gentry were more concerned with consolidating their estates than selling land. In any case land was expensive to buy, at least 20 times its annual value and this had to be paid as a lump sum in cash. An individual had to be very wealthy to find such amounts of money, and it was not easy to borrow large sums before the 1550s because of the Church's opposition to money lending. Furthermore, having acquired the land, a merchant or lawyer had to give up his former occupation and still have enough money to adopt the leisurely and lavish lifestyle of the gentry. Only a few succeeded in making the transition. Thomas Spring, a clothier from Lavenham in Suffolk (see page 45), was the third richest man in England outside London in 1522. He bought several manors in Suffolk, and his son, Sir John Spring, was readily accepted into the Suffolk gentry. At the same time he gave his daughter, Bridget, a large dowry when she married Aubrey de Vere, the Earl of Oxford. However, it was normally considered to take three generations to live down the stigma of trade. Because of the high cost of land, many of the wealthy trying to acquire status preferred to lease estates or, in the case of yeomen and husbandmen, just to buy single farms. Even so, by the middle of the century, before the newly confiscated monastic estates had become widely available, there was increasing pressure on the land. It is thought that this demand came not only from the existing gentry but also from successful merchants and lawyers, estate officials and from leasehold tenants and yeomen trying to convert their holdings into freehold. Evidence for such pressure comes from unsuccessful attempts in parliament to limit merchants from buying land worth over £50, clothiers more than £10 and yeomen and husbandmen in excess of £5.

4 The Mid-Tudor Elite Social Structure

Historians generally agree that by the 1550s the concept of the four orders in society was well established. However, the extent to which this indicated any real alteration in the structure of elite society is still open to debate. Clearly some significant changes had taken place since the fifteenth century and the elites had become more stratified. The old feudal concept that the king was *primus inter pares* (first among equals) or even *pares inter pares* (an equal among equals) with the nobility had disappeared. Tudor monarchs were seen as fathers of the commonwealth and were the social, as well as political, superiors of the old nobility. The peerage was now sharply defined into dukes, marquesses, earls, viscounts and barons. They were separated from the gentry by rank, the right to sit in the House of Lords and the legal privilege of being tried only by their equals. The gentry were also socially and legally divided into knights, esquires and gentlemen, although the distinction between the latter two was often blurred. At the same time the Reformation had drastically curtailed the political and economic power of the Church. This, by reducing the prestige of the higher clergy, enhanced the social and political position of both the nobility and the gentry.

Another consequence of the Reformation was the seizure of Church and monastic property with an annual value of some £3 million by the Crown. This reduced the power and prestige of the Church. Although some of this property was still held by the king in the 1550s, the granting or sale of the remainder influenced the social structure. Some historians consider that it was the nobility who were the initial beneficiaries from such sales and grants. Under Edward VI, the Dukes of Somerset and Northumberland, both of whom had risen from gentry families through the patronage of Henry VIII, received large amounts of ecclesiastical property. Somerset alone was given lands worth £12,000 a year while he was Lord Protector, which must be compared with the average noble income of £1,500. Other noble families with influence at court similarly enriched themselves on a smaller scale. By the 1550s it is still not absolutely clear to what extent this had helped the nobility to regain the economic position which they had lost as a result of the 'fourteenth-century crisis' (see page 7). Certainly many of their estates were still encumbered with long-term leases which would not run out until the end of the century. In any case, it was mainly those nobles sitting on the privy council who gained from the distribution of Church lands.

Similarly, it is difficult to assess how successful the gentry had been in exploiting this situation. Indeed, it is still not clear whether the 'rise of the gentry' was based on the acquisition of land and the commercial exploitation of their estates, or upon their ability to gain royal patronage. As the routes of upward social mobility were very varied, and the fortunes of individual families so diverse, historians find it difficult to be precise on this point. Another problem is to decide to what extent the other rising social groups – the yeomen, lawyers, merchants, industrialists and officials – had succeeded in integrating themselves into the elite structure through the acquisition of such land. In general terms there appears to have been no significant change in the landed social structure. At the beginning of the century there were 55 peers, 500 knights, 800 esquires and 5,000 gentlemen in the landed elites. These numbers remained fairly constant until the 1550s, although there may have been an increase in the lesser gentry. Many of the latter were younger sons, professionals and successful merchants and industrialists who were landless.

Possibly the easiest way of trying to resolve some of these issues is to examine changes within the county community. The landed elites were spread relatively evenly across the counties, apart from the nobility whose lands tended to be concentrated more in some areas than others. Taking north-west Berkshire as an example, it has been estimated that, in annual value, before the Reformation the Crown held some 8 per cent, the nobility 7 per cent, the Church 51 per cent, and the gentry 34 per cent of the land. This appears to have been fairly typical of the country as a whole. By 1550 this balance of land holding had changed significantly. The Crown held some 20 per cent, the nobility 6 per cent, the Church 12 per cent, the gentry 55 per cent and some had passed to the Oxford colleges. The change did not have as much of an impact on the structure of land holding as might have been expected. Of the 205 manors, 91 remained in the same ownerships and 114 changed hands, some of them several times. However, most of the land dealing was carried out by native gentry families, either to consolidate their existing holdings or to acquire more desirable manors. The overall picture is of consolidation and continuity. This did not give much scope for new entrants to acquire land. In all only nine manors passed into non-gentry hands. These were acquired by three London merchants, one local merchant, two local clothiers and one court official. This picture seems to confirm the view that it was difficult for the urban, professional and industrial elites to obtain land. Such a pattern appears to be typical for most of the county communities. Even in those adjacent to London, such as Kent, it was the native gentry families which were acquiring and continuing to hold land.

By the 1550s it is thought that there had been little significant alteration in the social structure. The first half of the century is seen as consolidating the changes begun in the fifteenth century. However, 1560 is recognised as marking the beginning of a new phase of social development which lasted until the middle of the seventeenth century.

5 Social Mobility 1560–1600

To a large extent the routes of elite social mobility did not change after 1560. Marriage and patronage continued to be the main avenues of social advancement. At the same time inflation, by raising land values, rent levels and prices, further enhanced the wealth of landowners and commercial groups. However, competition was becoming greater. The number of younger sons and daughters was increasing and more people from commerce and the professions were aspiring to elite status. It is considered that because of the favourable economic conditions, the elites were expanding more rapidly than the lower orders. Possibly the elites increased from 2 to 5 per cent of the population during the period. The average age of marriage for elite women is thought to have fallen from 24 to 20 or 21, while, in response to their falling standard of living, lower order women were marrying later, at the age of 27 or 28. For this reason elite families were producing on average 4.5 surviving children, while the remainder of the population was averaging only two. An example of such an increase is the Hyde family from Berkshire. William Hyde esquire, of Denchworth, left 13 surviving children when he died in 1557. In turn his eldest son had ten children. This meant that by the seventeenth century the younger Hyde children were in a variety of occupations ranging from the army, to bootmakers, innkeepers and drapers.

* At the same time there were variations in both the routes and perception of social mobility. The Church was no longer regarded as an ideal career for the sons of the landed elites. This change is reflected by the fact that the higher clergy during the reign of Elizabeth I were recruited mainly from the sons of yeomen and the urban and professional groups. On the other hand, the expansion of naval activity and overseas trade is seen as providing excellent career opportunities for younger sons. For example, John Hawkins and Francis Drake, who both came from Devon yeoman families, achieved fame and eminence at court by this means. Education and legal training became increasingly important for the gentry and the urban elites. However, it is thought that the nobility were less likely to send their sons to the grammar schools, universities and the Inns of Court, preferring the more traditional household training and tuition. Estate management, land conveyancing and marriage contracts were becoming increasingly complicated and legalistic after 1550. This made it necessary for even the eldest sons of the gentry to be educated and to have a basic legal training, if they were to keep their estates together in a more competitive society. Such considerations are thought to have been less important for the nobility because, with their greater resources, they could afford to employ lawyers and other household staff to manage their affairs. These developments meant that there was an ever growing range of career openings for younger sons with legal training at court, in central and local government and in the households of the landed and urban elites.

* Equally, the diversification of trade and industry made apprenticeship more attractive, even for the younger children of the gentry. This had the effect of making a commercial background more socially acceptable. Younger sons of gentlemen were beginning to be allowed to keep the status of their father even if they had followed a commercial career and owned no land. By 1600 only the strict purists among contemporary writers considered that it took three generations to remove the stigma of commercial origins. In some of the larger provincial towns, civic officials had begun to call themselves gentlemen and were sometimes legally given the title. It has been suggested that even by the end of the sixteenth century a new social group, which historians call the 'pseudo-gentry', was just beginning to emerge. Such people had the wealth, position and leisure to adopt an elite lifestyle, without owning the land which had previously been the necessary symbol of gentility. Possibly this was why the Elizabethan government re-enacted the sumptuary laws, in an unsuccessful attempt to stop social emulation by people of inferior status.

6 The Social Structure in 1600

There appears to have been great continuity in the structure of the Tudor landed elites, although the numbers at the lower end had increased. In 1500 it is estimated that there were 55 nobles, 800 esquires and some 5,000 gentlemen. By 1600 there were still 55 nobles, the number of knights had fallen to 350 and the number of esquires and gentlemen may have trebled. However, it must be remembered that social mobility was both upward and downward. Such apparent continuity conceals the constant turnover of landed families. The lavish lifestyle required by the elites frequently led to insolvency and bank-ruptcy. In addition, a common problem was the failure to produce a male heir, and the splitting up of estates between joint heiresses. During Elizabeth I's reign alone, 14 noble titles lapsed for this reason. Premature death, leaving an under-age heir, often led to royal wardship (whereby the estate was managed by Crown officials), resulting in a serious drain on the resources of the estate. Another constant danger was long-lived widows who were entitled to one-third of the estate for their lifetime. An ever present uncertainity was the vagary of royal favour, which could lead to the loss or restoration of titles and estates. The Percy family, Earls of Northumberland, is a good example of such varying fortune. In 1537 the title lapsed with the death of the 6th earl, and the estates passed to the crown (John Dudley, Lord President of the Council under Edward VI was made Duke of Northumberland in 1551, but this title lapsed when Dudley was executed in 1553). Mary I restored the earldom to Thomas Percy in 1557, but he was executed for treason in 1572. By the 1580s Henry Percy, the 9th earl, was deeply in debt, partly because of his long-lived mother. Then he married an heiress and his mother died; by 1600, helped by good estate manage-ment, he had doubled his income to £9,000 a year.

★ Apart from fluctuations of fortune for individual families, other changes were taking place within the county communities. The land market was still active. In north-west Berkshire a number of the smaller manors had been amalgamated in the process of estate consolidation. Out of the remaining 172 manors, 56 changed hands between 1550 and 1600. Half of these manors were acquired by new entrants to the landed elites. They consisted of five London merchants, two local clothiers, three former lessees, three local yeomen, two courtiers and a lawyer. This was a marked change from the 1550s, with the number of non-gentry entrants doubling. At the same time, some of them were wealthy enough to buy several manors. For example, by 1600 Thomas Parry, a Newbury clothier, had a holding of nine manors. This pattern seems to have been similar in most counties, with London merchants particularly active in the south-east. Further north, in Northampton-shire for example, new entrants were mainly local yeomen, lawyers and tradesmen from Northampton.

Although there were clear signs of change, it is thought that the overall picture is one of continuity. For example, of the 19 gentry families resident in north-west Berkshire in the 1520s, 16 were still there in 1600. During the century the number of resident families had risen to 44. This supports the idea that over the period the number of villages with a resident squire had risen from 10 per cent to 25 per cent, and is seen as significantly strengthening gentry influence within the counties. However, by 1600 the balance of power was beginning to change. In the 1520s the three leading county families, holding the major local offices, were the Fettiplaces, Essexes and Norreys, who had been established since the fifteenth century. The Fettiplaces lost royal favour because of their support for the Duke of Somerset in the power struggle following the death of Henry VIII. By the end the century they were falling into debt and having to sell off some of their manors. The Essex family fell heavily into debt because of over-generous bequests to charity and buying estates to give to younger children. By 1600 they were bankrupt, and an act of parliament was passed forcing them to sell their estates to pay off their creditors. In contrast, the Norreys family were very successful in their land dealings. Moreover, they gained royal favour under Elizabeth I and rose to become the Earls of Banbury in Oxfordshire. By 1600 their leading county role was being taken over by new rising families, such as the Untons, Pleydells and Garrards. However, although there was generally greater fluidity within landed society, it is considered that the real changes began to take place in the next century.

* Historians are broadly agreed that, while the outward structure of society appeared to be intact in 1600, a number of significant shifts were taking place within it. Society seems to have become more stratified. It has been suggested that there were six layers rather than four. At the top were the nobility. Then came the greater gentry, followed by the lesser elites. Beneath them were substantial and lesser yeomen, husbandmen, shopkeepers and tradesmen. Living-out labourers and cottagers in town and countryside came next. At the bottom were the unemployed, the old and infirm, widows, apprentices and servants, who formed 20 per cent of the population. However, this does not altogether clarify the position. It is relatively clear that the nobility and greater gentry, through their wealth, land and authority, formed the ruling elite. Equally evident is that the people in categories five and six were the lower orders, who were the ruled. The problem is how to classify those in the two middle groups.

* Like the other Tudors, Elizabeth I was anxious to preserve social stability. She kept the peerage at 55, and was equally careful to restrict the number of knights. During this period knighthood became recognised as a civil, rather than a military, honour. From the 1570s only some 20 knights a year were created to maintain the nucleus of local

government. It is considered that, although the nobility were given responsibilities as lords lieutenant of counties, they were generally under-employed administratively and at court. This, it is thought, enabled the greater gentry families to assume increased responsibility in local government. On the other hand, the economic position of some of the nobility had begun to improve. The average annual income of the nobles is estimated to have doubled during the century. In comparison, the income of knights had increased from an average of £130 a year to between £500 and £1000, that for esquires from £100 to £300, and for gentlemen from £14 to about £100. This indicates that the gentry had benefited more from the economic conditions than the nobility in general. Even with an inflation rate of 400 per cent, most of the gentry, unlike many of the nobility, were keeping pace, or ahead, of rising prices. However, by the end of the century, the long leases which had encumbered noble estates had expired. This meant that they could charge higher rents or take such land back into their own hands. It is considered that, with good estate management, the majority of the nobility, like the greater gentry, were in a strong economic position by 1600. Landed wealth still formed the solid base of family fortunes. Royal favourites and courtiers could rise to dizzy heights, but their success was usually ephemeral.

* The major problem of how to define the groups below the knights and esquires of the greater gentry and above the lower orders has puzzled both historians and contemporaries. Clearly the active land market after the Dissolution had led in an increase in the number of gentlemen holding one or two manors. These were the parochial gentry who held minor county offices. They have been described as the 'mere' gentry. Lacking royal patronage and the income from lucrative offices, they are seen as lacking the resources to maintain their status. Some came from ancient, established families, whilst others were new entrants from commerce and the law. Frequently they are virtually indistinguishable from prosperous yeomen. For example, when Henry Blagrove, yeoman, of Berkshire died in 1583 he left £341 in his will. At the same time his near neighbour, Philip Pusey, the head of a small, but ancient, gentry family, bequeathed only £238. From 1530 the College of Heralds, in an attempt to stop social emulation, conducted irregular visitations to the counties to check whether families had the right to the title that they had assumed. However, it is noticeable that many families who had been rejected earlier in the century were being given gentle status by the heralds by 1600. The debate on whether the 'mere' gentry were rising or falling will continue. What is clear is that by 1600 the land market was beginning to dry up. This is thought to have begun to put the lesser gentry under increasing pressure from the larger landowners. At the same time it meant that there was less land available for younger sons and new entrants.

1350 Late Feudal Society

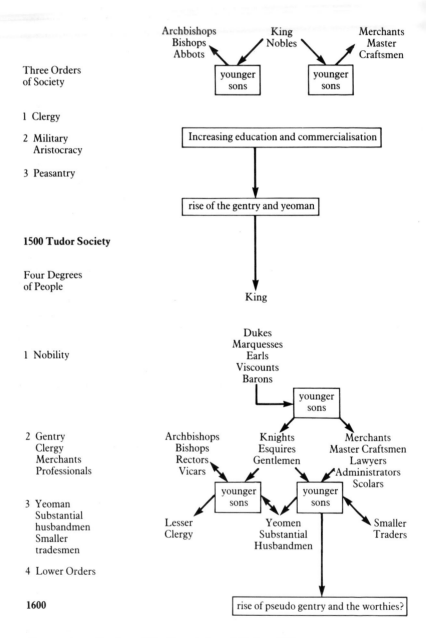

Three Orders
of Society

1 Clergy

2 Military
  Aristocracy

3 Peasantry

1500 Tudor Society

Four Degrees
of People

1 Nobility

2 Gentry
  Clergy
  Merchants
  Professionals

3 Yeoman
  Substantial
  husbandmen
  Smaller
  tradesmen

4 Lower Orders

1600

Summary – Society: The Landed and Urban Elites

The Commonwealth of England, 1565

1 Ordinarily the king does only make knights and create barons or
   higher degrees; for, as for gentlemen, they be made good cheap in
   England. For whosoever studies the laws of the realm, who
   studies at the universities, who professes liberal sciences and to be
5 short can live idly and without manual labour, and will bear the
   port, charge and countenance of a gentleman, he shall be called
   master, for that is the title given to esquires and other gentleman
   . . . [and in some cases they are given] arms newly made and
   invented, the title whereof shall pretend to have been found by
10 the said herald in perusing and viewing of old registers.

The problem remains as to how to classify the landless and professional groups within the elites. It is thought that by 1600 the higher
clergy had become equated with the greater gentry rather than the
nobility. On the other hand, the lower clergy had become better
educated, and many had maintained their incomes because inflation
had raised the value of their tithes and glebe land. For this reason it is
felt that they should be included amongst the lesser gentry. Some of the
wealthier merchants and lawyers in London had the power and lifestyle
to rank them alongside the nobility. In the provinces members of the
urban elites and professions had the prestige and wealth to mix on equal
terms with the county gentry. This process is thought to have been
helped because many towns were becoming social centres for the local
landed elites. The great difficulty is to draw the line separating the
growing numbers on the fringes of polite society from the lower orders.
It has been suggested that inflation and commercialisation was beginning to produce a materialistic, consumer society among the elites. For
this reason, the clearest social definition may rest on culture and
lifestyle (see chapter 8 for a fuller discussion of this aspect).

Making notes on 'Society: The Landed and Urban Elites'

Section 1 discusses the many theories and interpretations used by
historians to explain change in Tudor society. You need to have a clear
grasp of these in order to understand the historical debate. Refer back
to your notes on the theories about the 'fourteenth-century crisis' and
then note clearly how these are developed to explain what was
happening in the sixteenth century. At the same time, take care to
notice how more recent approaches, such as family and women's
history, are being used. It is important to have a good grasp of the social
models (both contemporary and modern) used to describe Tudor
society that are outlined in Section 2, but remember that these are very
simplified views of society. Section 3 discusses social mobility up to

1560. You have to be clear about the mechanisms and routes of social mobility, but remember that for most people mobility was more likely to be downwards than upwards. Social change is a very long-term process and it is thought that the Tudor elites went through two phases of transition, one between 1450 and the 1550s and another which started in 1560 and lasted until 1650. Section 4 examines the stage reached by elite society in the 1550s and you should make careful notes about its structure at this time. Section 5 considers how far the next phase of social mobility had reached by 1600 and you should note how this phase differed from the earlier one. Section 6 examines the stage that elite society had reached by 1600. Look carefully at the social structure in 1600 and identify the new landless elites, such as the 'pseudo-gentry'. Your notes should give a clear picture of the shape of society in 1450, 1500, 1550 and 1600. Be careful to note the changes taking place. Consider to what extent wealth was replacing land as the symbol of social status.

Source-based questions on 'Society: The Landed and Urban Elites'

1 Patronage
Carefully read the extracts from the two letters to Lady Lisle given on page 88. Answer the following questions.
a) What i) on the surface, and ii) in reality, was the writer of the first extract doing? (*4 marks*)
b) What was the writer of the second extract doing? What does this imply about the relationship between Thomas Warley and Lady Lisle? (*4 marks*)
c) How does the tone of the two extracts differ? Illustrate your answer with quotations from the extracts. (*6 marks*)
d) What was the likely social background of the priest mentioned in the second extract? Explain your answer. (*4 marks*)
e) Why would it have been important for Lady Lisle to respond positively to Thomas Warley's letter if she could? (*2 marks*)

2 Gentility
Carefully read the extract from 'The Commonwealth of England' given on page 97. Answer the following questions.
a) What does the writer describe as the main requirement for being regarded as a gentleman? (*2 marks*)
b) What is the author's opinion about this situation? Support your answer in detail. (*5 marks*)
c) What were the main reasons for the increase in the number of 'gentle' families in mid-Tudor England? (*3 marks*)
d) What were the effects of this increase? (*5 marks*)

CHAPTER 6

Society: Poverty and the Lower Orders

1 Introduction

It is just as difficult to generalise about the lower orders as it is about the social elites. The general theories (see page 76) all tend to represent change among this section of society as being a shift from peasant self-sufficiency to dependence upon wage labour. The predominant impression given is of large numbers of peasant smallholders being forced off the land to work for wages in the towns, so making way for large-scale commercial farmers.

Although it is true that by 1600 a significant number of smaller-scale husbandmen had left the land, such a picture is much too simplified. It conceals the great diversity in both the nature and the pattern of change to be found in different parts of the country (see page 13). At the same time, the lower orders seem to be represented as a very large, but essentially homogeneous, group. This again is misleading. There was considerable social stratification even among the peasant smallholders in the late middle ages, and these divisions increased during the sixteenth century. Equally, it must be remembered that a significant, and growing, proportion of the lower orders lived in towns and had their own hierarchy of status. Although there is much less evidence about the lower orders than about the elites, there has been a great deal of recent research in this area of study (see page 4). This has confirmed the complexity, and the local diversity, of social structuring to be found among these groups. At the same time it has revealed the difficulty of distinguishing between the bottom levels of the elites and the upper stratum of the lower orders.

* Theories and models can equally give distorted pictures of the amount of social and geographical mobility. An impression emerges that the lower orders were relatively static, although geographic mobility increased considerably during the sixteenth century. It now appears that this section of society was much more socially and geographically mobile than was previously thought. As was the case among the elites, primogeniture was widely practised (see page 15), while partible inheritance (the division of land among all the children) was the exception. This meant that most younger children left home in their early teens. The majority spent their adolescence in some form of training, either as apprentices or as servants in husbandry and industry. Those fortunate enough to secure apprenticeships are generally termed 'betterment' migrants, as they could be expected to improve their social

status. The others are seen as 'subsistence' migrants, because they were less likely to change their position in society. During this period the amount of such movement is considered to have increased because of population growth and the consequent pressure on the land. Although the numbers rising into the elites was small, there was constant movement upwards and downwards within the ranks of the lower orders themselves. Rapid demographic growth and inflation during the sixteenth century is seen as increasing this social mobility and as producing greater stratification. Rising prices and rents did not only create an ever-widening wealth gap between the elites and the non-elites, but also resulted in a similar polarisation among the lower orders themselves.

* Recently historians have been revising their ideas about the impact of poverty during this period. It is now thought that government intervention was not just a hurried response to cope with high levels of destitution in periods of bad harvests and unemployment. The Elizabethan poor laws are seen as the culmination of a long period of parliamentary legislation aimed at providing welfare for those unable to work and provide for themselves. At the same time, the laws are considered to have formed part of a government social policy (partially motivated by fear of disorder) which aimed to control, train and force the labouring masses into work. By 1600 it is thought that the system of parish relief was just about capable of supporting the impotent poor. This group, comprising pauper children, the old and the disabled, made up some 5 per cent of the population. However, the legislation was unsuccessful in dealing with the problem of vagrancy or fully providing for the 20 per cent of the population who were almost permanently living below the subsistence level by the end of the century. They were families willing to work but unable to find permanent employment. The impotent and the labouring poor came to form the bottom layer of the lower orders, and an ever widening gap grew between them and those fortunate enough to be in full employment.

The poor laws and other government legislation, such as the Statute of Artificers of 1563 (see page 52), are seen as a concerted attempt to order and discipline the non-elites. A sharp distinction began to emerge between employers, lesser yeomen, husbandmen and small craftsmen, and the remainder of the lower orders. Employers were increasingly given the task of organising the labouring masses. Masterless men were regarded with suspicion and seen as a threat to the social order. Such changes were reinforced by the English Reformation, which placed a greater emphasis on discipline and work ethics. The parish became the centre for government control through churchwardens and overseers of the poor. Central authority penetrated into the local community, thus changing the way of life of the villagers. Popular culture and customs (see page 125) began to be attacked by the educated elites and the

Church. This 'reformation of manners' is seen as a concerted effort by the authorities to convert the former independent peasantry into a docile, disciplined labour force.

2 Changes to the Social Structure 1350–1550

It is generally agreed that fundamental alterations within the peasantry began with the 'fourteenth-century crisis' (see page 5). Until then the basic structure of rural society had remained relatively stable, although there were local variations in different parts of the country. Peasant society is thought of as having been divided into four layers. At the top were freemen, who, unlike the remainder of the peasantry, were not serfs, and so did not belong to the lord of manor on which they lived. They paid their rent in cash or kind and did not have to perform labour services. Those holding land worth at least 40 shillings a year had the status of yeomen. However, many freemen held less land than this and were not as prosperous as many of their unfree neighbours. Below them came 'villeins', who generally held a yardland of 30 acres and were self-sufficient. A 'bordar' held a half yardland and was partially self-sufficient. At the bottom of rural society was the 'cottar', having a cottage and about five acres of land. Both bordars and cottars had to work for wages in order to supplement their income and achieve subsistence. Unlike freemen, villeins, borders and cottars were serfs and were legally the property of the lord of the manor on which they lived. They were not allowed to leave the manor without the permission of the lord and the payment of a fine in cash. They also had to obtain permission and pay a fine to get married. In addition to paying rent, they were expected to perform labour services on the lord's land. Normally this was for three days every week, with additional duties such as weeding the lord's corn and carting corn for a day. When a son inherited the smallholding he had to pay an 'entry fine', usually his 'best beast'.

All peasants were customary tenants. This meant that they held their land according to the customs of the manor on which they lived. These customs, together with the terms on which each tenant held his land, were recorded in a document (roll) which was held in the manorial court. The customs of each manor tended to be slightly different and developed over the centuries according to the social organisation and economic activity of the area. Frequently the extent of a manor was the same area as a parish, but this varied all over the country and sometimes there were several manors within one parish. In the south-eastern arable areas the centre of the manor was usually a compact village, whereas in the north and west settlements were more often scattered hamlets. Some manors were farmed on the traditional open three-field system, others were already enclosed and many had alternative practices, such as the two-field system common in northern England, depending upon their location. However, in all cases manors had common and waste land to which all customary tenants had access.

  * After 1350 a number of significant changes began to take place because of the greater availability of land and shifts in relationships between landlords and tenants (see page 6). Some of the more prosperous freemen and villeins took over vacant holdings to increase their landholdings to 60 or more acres. Similarly many of the half yardlanders acquired more land to become self-sufficient. On the other hand many of these former bordars were quite content to continue to farm some 30 acres and remain semi-self-sufficient. At the lower end of society many of the cottars abandoned their holdings to take advantage of the high wages created by the shortage of labour. Some went to work in areas of rural industry, while others migrated into towns. At the same time, a combination of shortage of tenants and peasant resistance forced the landlords to lower rents and to abandon many of their tenurial rights. By 1500 serfdom had virtually disappeared, and the greater part of the peasantry had become free. However, in various parts of the country some landlords continued to try to enforce their legal rights, particularly if their tenant was prosperous, as a means of increasing their income. In general by the sixteenth century most landlords had ceased to enforce labour services and control over marriage, and smallholders were free to move wherever they chose. Types of landholding also changed. Previously land had been either free or servile. By the end of the fifteenth century two new types of tenancy, copyhold and leasehold, had become more widespread. Copyhold had begun to replace customary tenancy in many places. Under this type of lease the holder was given a document which was a copy of the entry of the conditions of tenancy recorded on the manorial roll. Supposedly this gave the tenant greater legal protection under common law, although it was not recognised in all parts of the country. Copyhold tenure spread quickly during the sixteenth century, although there were still many customary tenants. A copyhold was hereditary, and was usually granted for three lives (until the death of the husband, wife and eldest son) or 21 years. The entry fine was normally equivalent to the annual rent, but this, and the amount of rental, varied from manor to manor. Leasehold was not hereditary, but was legally binding. In many cases the terms of the lease were adjustable annually. This led to 'rack renting', whereby the rent was increased every year so that the landlord could share in the profits of rising prices. Theoretically rents were reduced in times of harvest failure or trade slumps. Social distinction between types of landholding began to disappear. Yeomen and gentry frequently held land as freehold, leasehold and copyhold. Indeed, by 1600 copyhold land was regarded as freehold in some areas.

  * By the 1520s the lower orders had begun to adjust to these changes, and by the middle of the century the new structure was well established. At the beginning of the fourteenth century the population of the

village of Stanford in the Vale (see page 16) had consisted of 10 freemen, 48 villeins, 15 bordars and 5 cottars. In 1522 there were 6 freeholders, 1 yeoman, 23 substantial husbandmen, 11 husbandmen, 9 cottagers and 8 servants in husbandry. A yeoman would generally have held over 60 acres and be farming commercially, employing servants in husbandry and wage labourers from among the cottagers in the village. Husbandmen are thought to have held between 5 and 60 acres of land. Those with the larger holdings would have farmed commercially and employed servants and other labour, while those with the smaller amounts of land would not have been fully self-sufficient and would have had to supplement their incomes with other work. The cottagers supplied labour for their neighbours, but were partially self-sufficient from the produce of their gardens and whatever they could glean from the commons, waste and woodlands. The villagers at Stanford still appear to have been customary tenants in 1522. The six freeholders held only small plots of land besides their tenancies. Four of them were less substantial husbandmen and the other two were cottagers. There were comparatively few servants and labourers in the village. However, in areas of rural industry they could form about 40 per cent of the population. There had been some social differentiation in Stanford, with a growing wealth gap between the yeoman and substantial husbandmen at the top and the cottagers at the bottom. Yet, in general, the village community was relatively egalitarian, with all its members involved, more or less independently, in its farming activities. This situation was true for a large majority of the rural parishes and for many towns. The term 'householder' was used to denote those people with a permanent home, as opposed to the masterless vagrant. The authorities regarded the householder in both town and country as the 'better sort' of respectable society. They were the people who paid taxes and were potential employers who contributed towards the prosperity of the commonwealth. Officially in 1522 the villagers of Stanford were all regarded as respectable householders of equal status despite disparities in wealth.

   * It might be expected that there would be a noticeable difference between those living in the countryside and town dwellers. However, in the sixteenth century they were all described as householders, husbandmen, apprentices, servants and labourers. Wealth levels in towns tended to be higher, but there were many country yeomen and husbandmen who were just as rich. Alternative sources, such as inventories, reveal that urban yeomen and husbandmen were often tanners, mercers, shoemakers or carpenters. However, some of the country yeomen and husbandmen were clothiers, or were mainly engaged in industrial activities. It must not be thought that yeomen and husbandmen were exclusively farmers. At the same time, even in quite large towns, many people were engaged in agricultural occupations. In the early sixteenth century all these people were clearly regarded as

members of the lower orders. However, as the century progressed it becomes increasingly difficult to decide where to draw the line between the top of the lower orders and the bottom levels of the elites (see page 97).

3 The Family, Marriage and Social Mobility

Once it was maintained by historians and anthropologists that the English peasantry closely resembled modern peasant societies. In particular it was thought that the English family was 'extended' to include grandparents, in-laws and married brothers and sisters. This view is no longer widely held. It is now thought that most lower order families were 'nuclear', and consisted of the parents, children and possibly a surviving grandparent. Extended families were more likely to be found in the large households of the nobility, where it was common for married younger children to live at home until they had the opportunity (if ever) to set up their own establishments. At the same time it was once thought that villages were mainly made up of closely related families. This was seen as giving rise to close-knit, kinship-linked communities, where families lived for generations. Recent research has suggested that this was not normally the case. Analysis of taxation lists and parish registers has revealed that there was a surprisingly rapid turn-over of families in the villages as well as in the towns. It is thought that up to 30 per cent of the inhabitants might move from a village every ten years. Such movement was not limited to single younger children, but also included whole families of cottagers and husbandmen. It was only the yeomen and substantial husbandmen who were likely to stay in the same place for several generations. This meant that there was considerable underlying mobility among the lower orders which increased as economic conditions deteriorated during the second half of the century.

   * In the countryside it was usual for the eldest son to stay at home and to inherit the family holding on his father's death. Sometimes he married during his father's life time, but generally marriage was delayed until after inheritance. Younger brothers and sisters stayed at home until their early teens. From the age of about six they were expected to work on the family smallholding until they left for service or apprenticeship. The younger children of cottagers were expected to work at spinning or some other form of industry in order to contribute to the family economy. They were all expected to train as servants in husbandry, unless they were apprentices, or worked in specialist occupations, such as mining or seafaring. In woodland-pasture regions and parts of Kent, partible inheritance was more common. The constant subdivision of smallholdings among all the children meant that they quickly became too small to provide subsistence. As a result, in

these areas the population became increasing dependent upon employment in rural industry.

* Yeomen and the more substantial husbandmen and craftsmen could afford to provide good education and training for their children, although some still became servants in husbandry. Most sons were sent to the growing number of grammar and free schools being established in towns and countryside (see page 139). In the second half of the century more of them went on to university and some to the Inns of Court. This opened up a wide range of career prospects in central and local government, the professions and the households of the elites. Training for the Church became increasingly popular and by 1600 the majority of the higher clergy in the Church of England had come from a yeomen background. The more traditional route of apprenticeship was followed by many seeking to profit from the growth and diversification of industry. At the same time, the expansion of overseas trade offered attractive career openings for younger sons from this group.

The prospects for daughters were less promising. Marriage was becoming more important as a means of improving a family's social position. However, unlike those among the landed elites, arranged marriages were not common and many daughters appear to have played some part in choosing their future husbands. Education was considered to be less important for girls. Few apparently went even to the free elementary schools, much less to the grammar schools. A number were still apprenticed into a variety of trades, but there is evidence of growing male opposition to women apprentices. To a large extent it appears that the daughters from these groups were destined for marriage, childbearing and household management.

These developments had the effect of increasing stratification among the lower orders. Education was seen to be an increasingly important mark of social status, giving access to a growing number of career opportunities. A gulf was beginning to develop between the educated top ranks of the lower orders and the largely illiterate masses below them. These educated people began to identify themselves with the elites and to disassociate themselves from the cottagers and wage earners. At the same time lack of education is thought to have lowered the status of women and to have inflated male superiority. It has been calculated that by 1600 only some 10 per cent of women were literate, as opposed to some 75 per cent of men among the landed and urban elites. As a result women are judged to have been marginalised in the workplace and subordinated in the home.

* Although levels of lower order illiteracy have been estimated to have been over 90 per cent by 1600, it appears that growing numbers were taking advantage of the availability of free elementary education. Not only were some of the less prosperous husbandmen, craftsmen and even cottagers sending children to school, but there is evidence of self-education among farm workers and labourers. The growing pub-

lication and sale by travelling pedlars and chapmen of popular ballads and almanacs suggests the beginnings of a mass market. The trend towards mass literacy was helped by the emphasis by the Church of England and puritan reformers on education and the need for everyone to be able to read the Bible. However, by the 1580s worsening economic conditions meant that few of the less prosperous households could afford to allow their children to attend even free schools because of the cost of books and other materials. In any case, the children were required to work to supplement the family income. Similarly, lack of finance made it difficult for these families to apprentice their children into trades, although by the end of the century there were a growing number of pauper apprenticeships (see page 116). Smaller scale husbandmen and craftsmen, along with wage labourers, were falling into a poverty gap of inflation, diminishing wages and a shortage of employment, particularly in years of harvest failure or trade slump.

* Most younger children from these groups went into some form of service in husbandry or industry. This was the form of training approved of by the authorities and laid down in the Statute of Artificers of 1563. Servants formed the core of the permanent wage force. They were hired by the year, generally at the Michaelmas fairs, and paid at the rate laid down annually by the county justices of the peace. They then became part of the family of their employer and the head of the household became responsible for their training, moral education and welfare. They ate with the family and were provided with clothes, which meant that they could save their wages in preparation for marriage in their mid-twenties. Recent research has shown that most servants generally moved annually to another household to learn new skills. It has been estimated that, on average, they travelled a distance of about 17 kilometres a year to find another place to work. Men and women shared equally in the work, although in agriculture ploughing and carting were male occupations, while women specialised in dairying. However, it has been suggested that by the end of the period commercial farming and increased technology might have been beginning to undermine the role of women at work. Reductions in labour made it more difficult for women to find well paid jobs in agriculture. Similarly, women and children were increasingly being relegated to low paid spinning and carding in the textile industries. This meant that women's potential contribution to the family economy fell. Alongside the impact of inflation on living standards, this is seen as forcing up the age of marriage among the lower orders.

* Even so, lower order women had more independence over marriage than their counterparts in the elites. Most parents in this group had little or no property and selecting the right marriage partner was of less legal importance. As their daughters were unlikely to receive any dowry, parental opinions and consent were not highly regarded. In any case most of them left parental control in their early teens and rarely

returned home apart from visits. Betrothal and marriage were much freer than among the elites. The authorities preferred marriage in church with a proper calling of the banns, but a large proportion of lower order marriages are thought not to have been solemnised in church.

The Church recognised verbal consent to marriage in the present tense before witnesses to be legally binding. Consent in the future tense, provided that it was followed by sexual intercourse, was equally legal. Such 'hand troth' marriages were common. In the frequent absence of parents, advice from friends appears to have been important in the choice of marriage partners. Analysis of marriage and baptismal registers shows that there was a very high percentage of prenuptial pregnancy. This appears to have been widespread and socially acceptable. It seems to have been usual practice for young couples to sleep together after betrothal. In any case it was common for male and female servants to share the same bed. When daughters were still living at home, the custom of 'bundling' required the girl's parents to provide a betrothed couple with a bed until they married or set up a separate establishment.

At this level the of amount of upward mobility was very limited because most young couples were marrying their social equals. However, girls in service did quite often marry apprentices who, being skilled craftsmen, had the opportunity of moving up the social scale. Marriage was very much an economic and social necessity. The authorities regarded single people with suspicion and frequently associated them with vagrancy (see page 110). Furthermore, the deteriorating economy during the period made it almost impossible for an individual to subsist outside the combined incomes of a marriage. This is why re-marriage generally followed very quickly if either partner died.

4 Poverty and Vagrancy

There has been considerable debate about poverty and vagrancy. It is agreed that inflation, worsening economic conditions and demographic increase were the basic underlying causes of the problem. Equally, the closure of the monasteries, unemployment in the textile industry, harvest failures, enclosure and increased numbers of discharged service men and retainers are all thought to have contributed to the problem. However, many of the previous assumptions have been revised. The myth that some 80,000 monks, nuns, retainers, servants and tenants were displaced to join the ranks of the needy by the dissolution of the monasteries has long been dismissed. The former inmates were given pensions and generally found new employment, while the tenants continued to farm under new private owners. What is now being re-examined is the nature of the poor. It had been assumed that the poor formed themselves into large bands of professional, and potentially criminal, vagabonds who roamed the countryside (a view often taken by the Tudor authorities). The presence of groups of soldiers and sailors discharged at the end of military campaigns was seen as adding an extra element of violence. The long-term poor were considered to have formed the nucleus of a widespread criminal underworld. Many poor families were thought to have adopted a life of petty crime and vagabondage on the fringes of society. While it is agreed that this might have been true in a minority of cases, the overall picture is considered to have been very different. Most vagrants are thought to have been young single people, male and female, who were genuinely looking for work. Labouring families were generally settled, but could be thrown into poverty by harvest failure, trade slumps or illness. Although there was crime, it is now considered to have been mainly petty pilfering in dearth years, rather than the work of organised gangs of criminals.

Equally there are doubts about the extent and nature of private charity and hospitality. It is now considered that such changes had begun by 1500, rather than being caused by the Reformation. The great households were already in decline and this reduced the amount of free hospitality offered to the needy. In any case, the elites were beginning to develop a greater desire for privacy. Humanistic thought emphasised moderation and good taste, as opposed to lavish entertainment. It also brought a change of attitude towards poverty, which was fostered by the Reformation. There was a growing recognition that the impotent poor should be supported by the state. At the same time the authorities became increasingly opposed to the indiscriminate donation of private charity. The poor became divided into the deserving and the undeserving. The authorities felt that the former should be provided for out of parish funds, while the latter should be put to work. It was once thought that levels of private charity rose over the period. However, while it is true that the size of bequests increased and almshouses continued to be established, it is now considered that, once inflation is taken into account, amounts actually decreased. Moreover, the monastic and private hospitals and almshouses closed down at the time of the Reformation had not been replaced by the end of the period. Monastic alms alone are calculated to have amounted to about £65,000 a year, while public and private charity together totalled only some £45,000 by 1600.

* Reactions by Tudor governments to the poverty problem used to be seen as panic measures adopted in years of particular economic difficulty. It is now thought that by the end of the century they were trying to establish a coherent welfare policy, although provision barely met demand even in normal years. The overall problem was that the standard of living for the great majority of people fell drastically during the period (see page 29). Increasing centralisation meant that the state had to assume responsibility for charity provision previously catered for by the Church and private individuals. It had always been the christian

duty of the rich and powerful to care for the needs of the poor and weak. Humanistic thought (see page 150) regarded indiscriminate hospitality as wasteful. The concept of charity became separated from what had once been the pious duty of providing food and hospitality in the home for passing travellers or the local poor. The home and family is seen as becoming much more private. In any case, by the 1580s the worsening economic conditions are seen to have brought a breakdown in neighbourliness and a growing mistrust of strangers (see page 129). Provision for the poor became a public, rather than a private, function, and as such was part of the government's general social control legislation.

* It is difficult to account for the apparent increase in poverty because there were so many and varied possible reasons and there is very little agreement among historians. Although there is no doubt that living standards among the lower orders had declined by 1600, doubts have been expressed about whether this was the underlying reason for the passing of the poor laws. In the 1520s 30 per cent of the population were too poor to tax, and it is doubtful whether the proportion was much higher in normal years by the end of the period. Even so, the rapid increase in population meant that there were greater numbers of poor to be catered for. At the same time the distribution of the population was changing, with more people moving into towns, particularly after the 1570s. This was clearly making it more difficult for local authorities to deal with the problem. In the countryside population growth was resulting in growing numbers of cottagers who were no longer self-sufficient and therefore less able to support themselves. At the same time there was a movement away from the arable parishes of the south into the open pastoral parishes of the Midlands and the north. There were normally a few poor families, frequently widows, amounting to about 3 per cent of the population in every parish. While rural and urban parishes could cope with this situation, they could not cater for growing numbers of poor cottagers and fluctuating numbers of migrant workers.

Another possible explanation of the problem is that the nature of poverty was altering. This may have been the result of social and economic change creating new difficulties, or just that old ones were being made worse. It is thought that there were two basic types of poverty by the end of the period. The impotent poor, or paupers, represented deep poverty. This group was typically made up of the very young and the old, and comprised 5 per cent of the urban population and slightly less in the country parishes. It consisted of widows and widowers, deserted wives and broken families with young children, and some of the unemployed adolescents. Working women, because their low wages were usually well below subsistence, were particularly vulnerable if they were deserted or if their husband died. By the end of the century population growth meant that Tudor England had a very young population. It is estimated that 40 per cent of the population were children and that about 45 per cent of the poor were below the age of 10. This meant that the problem of deep poverty was expanding, and it was to help this group of 'deserving poor' that the law aimed. At the same time, the number of the 'shallow' poor was also increasing. They comprised the rapidly growing number of cottagers and labouring families living on the very edge of subsistence. A bad harvest, a trade slump causing temporary unemployment, injury or illness could easily plunge such families into poverty. In bad years hardship among this group could raise the basic numbers of the poor from 5 per cent to 20 per cent. In addition, many other families had scarcely enough income to buy food and other necessities, which brought them perilously close to the poverty line.

It is agreed that the extent of Tudor poverty may well have increased in depth and numbers. However, some historians consider that the Tudor poor laws came as a result of a change of attitude, rather than because of the size of the problem. This view takes into account the extent to which a society feels an obligation to provide for its less able members. Thomas More was expressing the ideal humanistic view in *Utopia* when he envisaged a society where the impotent poor were cared for by the state and all the able-bodied given the chance to work. To a large extent this was reflected in government action. By the end of the century the deserving poor were largely catered for by parish relief. The authorities took the view that the able bodied should be put to work. Unfortunately, it was considered that all those who were not in work were idle and undeserving. Little recognition was given to the fact that the majority of the unemployed were seeking work but that there were no jobs available. In this respect the poor laws formed part of the general economic legislation centred around the Statute of Artificers of 1563, which aimed to ensure that all the lower orders between the ages of 12 and 60 should be in some form of employment or training. Another aspect of this was the attitude that everyone should have a master and be part of a household. Consequently single and masterless men and women were regarded as dangerous and a threat to social stability. This became increasingly true during the second half of the century. The receipt of poor relief became linked with the obligation to work, while the vagrant was regard as a rebellious criminal who had to be punished.

* Behind the official attitude to vagrants was the assumption that they were trying to evade work rather than seeking employment. At the same time contemporaries were convinced that they were a threat to social order, health and morality. The itinerant poor were seen as dirty, contagious carriers of disease who were responsible for outbreaks of plague. They were thought to be thieves and outlaws who were guilty of spreading seditious rumours. Above all they were regarded as sinful and as full of vice and lust as the wild animals. Such attitudes

marginalised vagrants and set them outside the fringes of society. Any of these claims may well have been true of a few individuals, at times, in some places. However, most historians consider that they were grossly exaggerated, and reflect local problems and tensions particularly after the 1580s. It is now thought that vagrants were a typical cross-section of the lower orders. Mostly they were young and single between the ages of 15 and 25. Men predominated, but 25 per cent are thought to have been women. By 1600 they may well have represented 2 per cent of the population. In general they seem to have been younger children who had been unable to find employment in service or apprenticeship and had been forced to move to seek work because of increasing population pressure. They are seen as being divided into those who were moving into towns, and those migrating into the more industrial open parishes (see page 109). Vagrants of this type were usually long term and covered long distances of over 50 miles a year. Frequently they had fixed itineraries between temporary employment; spending the summer in the countryside and seeking more permanent shelter in a town during the winter.

The government reacted to the increasing size of this problem by trying to force all itinerants to return to their place of birth. Anyone caught without a passport, or licence to travel, was liable to punishment. In practice this was difficult to enforce and local authorities were often lax. The problem was compounded because large numbers of often legitimate travellers were caught up in the legislation. Actors, musicians, acrobats, discharged soldiers and sailors, servants, apprentices, peddlers and chapmen could all fall foul of the law. Many of them might well have been travelling between fairs and other places of popular entertainment, but so were many of the migrant workers. Discharged service men could have been making their way home. Apprentices and servants might have been going to their next employer, or equally they could have been running away from their place of work. Such problems made any legislation virtually unenforceable.

5 The Tudor Poor Laws

Poor law legislation can be seen as falling into two phases. Up to the 1570s the measures were haphazard and uncoordinated. Then an increasingly systematic policy was adopted, which culminated in the Poor Law of 1601. There has been some debate as to whether urban authorities or the government were most instrumental in shaping poor law policy. It is now generally agreed that, although urban experiments in poor relief provided valuable experience, central government initiated the main policy thrust through parliamentary legislation. This is seen as part of the general Tudor policy of strengthening central control. Responsibility for the poor was placed firmly on the parish. The administration of relief passed into the hands of the churchwardens

Poverty

and overseers of the poor appointed by the local justices. This is seen as yet a further example of government intrusion into the traditional community (see page 126).

   * Prior to the establishment of the poor laws, any relief, apart from that provided by the monasteries and private charity, was very haphazard. No differentiation was made between the impotent and the able-bodied poor. Most local authorities allowed paupers (the infirm, the old and children) to beg, and in many towns they were issued with special badges. The urban guilds and charitable fraternities provided welfare for their own members. In the countryside parish constables and officials of the manorial court often organised supplementary relief. For this purpose they drew upon the church poor box to provide help for genuinely needy travellers and for any village family with particular problems. However, in general each community depended on cooperation among neighbours to care for its own resident destitute, and relied on the authorities to help drive away unwanted strangers. This situation

was reinforced by the earliest Tudor legislation, the Vagrancy Act of 1495. The act ordered that all itinerants were to be rounded up, placed in the stocks for three days and then sent home. At the same time local authorities were instructed to ensure that paupers only begged within the district of their birth.

  * Until the 1560s this position remained virtually unchanged. In the 1520s a run of bad harvests (see page 17) caused bread shortages in many towns, and the situation was made worse by a slump in cloth sales which caused widespread unemployment in areas of textile manufacture. Some towns, such as Norwich and Exeter, introduced a new policy of laying in stocks of grain to feed the poor in times of dearth. The government's main concern was still depopulation caused by the conversion of arable land to pasture, and what was seen as the increasing problem of vagrancy. However, the poor act of 1531 is seen as a response to the economic difficulties of the late 1520s. The main thrust of the legislation was against vagabonds, who were ordered to be rounded up in every parish, whipped and sent back to their place of origin. Importantly, a distinction was made for the first time between the impotent and the able-bodied poor, although it was still assumed that the able-bodied could find work if they looked for it. No actual provision was made for paupers, but licensed begging and the wearing of a badge was extended to the whole country.

The issue continued to be discussed in parliament and a new bill was drafted. It was proposed to introduce a form of income tax to finance parish relief for the aged and infirm, and to provide an apprenticeship scheme for pauper children. At the same time, public works, such as road building, were to be set up to give employment to the able-bodied poor. However, in the proposed new act of 1536 (which was not passed by parliament) most of these provisions had disappeared because many MPs were opposed to the additional taxation. Instead, instructions were issued that begging was to be curbed, and that parishes were to become responsible for the impotent poor. Money for this purpose was to be raised by voluntary subscriptions by parishioners, and private almsgiving was to cease. Pauper children were to be put into service or apprenticeship. No help was to be given to the able-bodied poor. Indeed, monthly searches were to be made for vagrants, who were to be sent home, and persistent offenders could be hanged. By the 1540s growing popular unrest made the government increasingly fearful of widespread disorder. This led to the passing of the savage Vagrancy Act of 1547. It was ordered that any able-bodied person out of work for more than three days was to be branded with a 'V' and sold into slavery for two years. Persistent offenders were to become permanent slaves. Vagrant children were to be taken from their parents and apprenticed into useful trades. This act was universally unpopular and was ignored by the local authorities. It was repealed in 1550, and the 1531 act again briefly came into force.

* However, after the mid-century disorders, a new piece of poor law legislation was introduced in 1552. The provisions of the proposed act of 1536 for the relief of the impotent poor were revived. Parishioners were to be invited to make weekly voluntary payments in church, and registers were to be kept of both the poor and the subscribers. This act was repealed in 1555, and licensed begging was again allowed in areas of high poverty. There appear to have been several reasons why it was so difficult to put any coherent poverty policy into force. Parliament favoured a system of parish relief, but there was widespread resistance to the replacement of private charity by public provision based on compulsion. In any case, the government seemed more concerned with suppressing vagrancy than in aiding the poor. The town authorities, faced with the problem of large numbers of unemployed migrants, favoured a policy of centralised municipal relief.

While parliament and the government wavered, London and some of the larger towns took decisive action. Following the closure of monastic hospitals in London, the authorities persuaded Henry VIII to give St Bartholomew's, Christ's and St Thomas's hospitals to the city, and subsequently bought Bridewell and Bedlam for £2,000. They were reorganised under boards of civic governors; St Bartholomew's and St Thomas's were used to house the sick and elderly, children and vagrants were sent to Christ's and Bridewell and the insane went to Bedlam. In 1547 compulsory payment was imposed on London householders to pay for this system of outdoor relief.

Guild Hall Journal, 1547

1 For as much as the late order lately divised and taken by the lord
  mayor and aldermen for the relief, maintenance and funding of
  the poor, sick and indigient persons appointed to be found and
  kept within the house and hospital lately erected and founded by
5 the most noble prince of famous memory king Henry the eighth
  . . . the costs and charges to the citizens and inhabitants of this
  city [from] the profits and revenues of such lands and tenements
  as his highness endowed the same house [and from] charitable
  alms of the people weekly to be gathered within the parish
10 churches [is insufficient]. It is therefore for the remedy and
  support thereof this day by the lord mayor, aldermen and
  commons in this present common council assembled and authority of the same ordained, enacted, granted and established that
  the citizens and inhabitants of the said city shall forthwith
15 contribute and pay towards the sustenance, maintaining and
  funding of the said poor personages.

Other towns also began to set up similar hospitals to cope with the growing number of poor migrants. After the 1570s, many of these 'houses of correction', which became known as 'bridewells', were established where able-bodied vagrants were set to work. Compulsory payments were introduced in Norwich in 1549 and in York in 1550, and other towns began to adopt the same policy. At Norwich and other towns regular censuses of the poor were carried out and a system of provision established.

* Despite these urban advances, the government still wavered about introducing compulsory payments toward poor relief. The 1563 poor act laid down only that lists of parishioners refusing to contribute were to kept, and that persistent non-payers could be fined and imprisoned. Moreover, the amount to be paid was not specified. This legislation, together with the Act of Artificers, was very haphazardly enforced by the local authorities. It was only after the Northern Rebellion of 1569, which created fresh fears about disorders, that the government took decisive action. The acts of 1572 and 1576 finally established the principle of compulsory weekly payments (according to need) for poor relief by parishioners.

Act Directing the Levy of a Compulsory Poor Rate, 1572
1 . . . And when the number of the said poor people forced to live
   upon alms be by that means truly known, the said justices,
   mayors, sheriffs, bailiffs and other officers shall (as soon as
   convenient) devise and appoint, within every [of] their said
5 divisions, meet [proper] and convenient places by their discre-
   tions to settle the same poor people for their habitations and
   abidings, if the parish within the which they shall found shall not
   or will not provide for them; and shall also within the like
   convenient time number [count] all the said poor people within
10 their said several [various] limits [boundaries], and thereupon
   (having regard the number) set down what portion the weekly
   charge towards the relief and sustenance of the said poor will
   amount to within every [of] their several divisions and limits; and
   that done, they . . . shall by their good discretion tax and assess
15 all and every [of] the inhabitants . . .

A full survey of the poor was to be made by local JPs. Four overseers were to be selected by the local justices from substantial householders (yeomen, husbandmen and tradesmen) to help the churchwardens and parish constables in the administration. At the same time, the laws against vagabonds were strengthened. Vagrants were to be rounded up and brought before the courts. Culprits were to have a hole bored in their ear, and be sent home after being whipped 'until bloody'. If necessary, each parish was to build a house of correction, and keep stocks of wool, hemp and iron, where the able-bodied would be set to work. However, some recognition was made that some vagrants were actually seeking work, and itinerant harvest workers and migrant servants were no longer to be penalised.

* Once again these provisions were very haphazardly applied, particularly as a run of particularly good harvests (see page 20) eased worries about disorder and food shortages. In 1593 the laws against vagrants were eased so that in future they would be only whipped and sent home. At the same time, the favourable conditions enabled the government to press ahead with legislation on social and economic regulation. In part this was aimed at imposing greater discipline and a 'reformation of manners' among the lower orders (see page 117). Several laws were passed to curb swearing and drunkenness, and to restrict the activities of ale houses. Attempts were made to improve hygiene and health and control plague outbreaks by quarantining whole families in their houses for six weeks until the danger of infection had passed. Town and country authorities were encouraged to build up stocks of grain and to establish procedures for distribution and price regulation in dearth years (see page 22). These measures, and a whole range of earlier legislation, were brought together in books of orders, which were up-dated and regularly sent out to local authorities for them to implement. The first, issued in 1578, dealt largely with public health, while the second, produced in 1586 (when harvest yields had begun to fall), was concerned with grain distribution and poor relief.

* The harvest failures and crises of the mid-1590s brought a renewed burst of government action. Food riots, associated mainly with anti-enclosure disorder, brought renewed legislation against enclosure in 1598. In the same year, after considerable debate in parliament, a new poor law was introduced. This largely reinforced the 1572 act. Compulsory provision for the impotent poor was confirmed, which was to be provided through taxes on landowners and householders. Pauper apprenticeships were to be set up for poor children; boys to be trained until the age of 24 and girls until 21. Parish constables were to be in charge of rounding up vagrants, whipping them and returning them to their place of origin. More houses of correction were to be built where the able-bodied were to be set to work. Overseers had to keep annual accounts and ensure that there was no begging. At the same time, commissions were set up to investigate private charitable trusts and endowments, and make it easier for individuals to establish almshouses and hospitals. The act acknowledged that private, as well as public, charity was an essential part of poor relief. The 1601 act confirmed these measures. A few minor adjustments were made. Pauper girls were allowed to leave apprenticeship before the age of 21 if they married, and the number of overseers was reduced from four to two. Many local authorities continued to resist what they saw as central government interference, and the legislation was often difficult to enforce. However, with some adjustments, the 1601 act became the basis of poor relief provision for the next two centuries.

There is still much debate on the reasons for and the achievements of Tudor poor law legislation. It is now generally agreed that parliament and the government were trying to tackle on a national level the problem of what they saw as genuine poverty. However, this is seen as forming part of the privy council's strategy to exert greater central control and to reduce the power of local government. To a large extent the government was only partially successful in imposing such control and the urban and county authorities continued to exercise considerable independence. The result was that there were great variations in the way in which counties, towns and individual parishes interepreted and implemented the poor laws. Indeed, the disparities in levels of relief and the treatment of the poor make it very difficult to come to any general conclusion about the overall success of the legislation. In broad terms it is thought that the impotent poor, impoverished widows, widowers, children and the infirm, were generally satisfactorily provided for by the end of the century. Equally, the labouring poor received some relief in dearth years. Where the legislation failed was in dealing with the linked problems of unemployment and vagrancy. Even by 1600 the privy council had not come to terms with the problem that the young and able-bodied could not find employment if work was not available. This meant that the government's aim to impose greater discipline and social control over the unruly masses was only partially achieved (see page 126).

6 The Lower Order Social Structure by 1600

Although there was no significant change in the pattern of lower order social mobility during the period, there was a marked shift in the structure itself. The main reason for this was population growth and inflation which created ever more virtually landless cottagers in both town and countryside. At the same time, increased commercialism among yeomen and husbandmen meant that the wealth gap between the top and bottom of the non-elites had steadily widened. This polarisation was made more pronounced by the educational, legal, religious and cultural developments of the period. The top ranks of the lower orders began to associate themselves increasingly with the attitudes of the elites and the government.

This is what makes it so difficult to distinguish where the bottom of the elites ends and the top of the lower orders begins. Yeomen, substantial husbandmen and self-employed craftsmen and tradesmen became recognised as part of the 'better sort'. They were the householders and employers who were expected by the government to impose order and discipline on the unruly masses. Inflation and market forces brought them greater affluence and they were able to benefit from the educational opportunities and growing material comfort of the period. This in turn meant that they began to conform to the humanistic ideals of rationality and good taste, and away from the unruly boisterousness of popular culture (see page 127). While this had been true for some

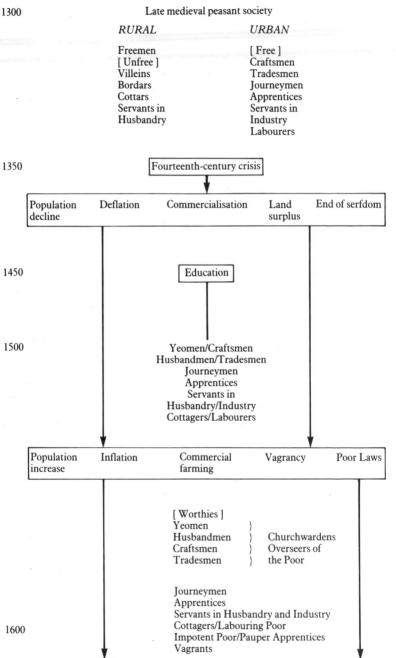

1300   Late medieval peasant society

               RURAL   URBAN

               Freemen   [Free]
               [Unfree]   Craftsmen
               Villeins   Tradesmen
               Bordars   Journeymen
               Cottars   Apprentices
               Servants in   Servants in
               Husbandry   Industry
                                                   Labourers

1350   Fourteenth-century crisis

       Population   Deflation   Commercialisation   Land   End of serfdom
       decline   surplus

1450   Education

1500   Yeomen/Craftsmen
                                 Husbandmen/Tradesmen
                                      Journeymen
                                      Apprentices
                                      Servants in
                                 Husbandry/Industry
                                 Cottagers/Labourers

       Population   Inflation   Commercial   Vagrancy   Poor Laws
       increase   farming

                           [Worthies]
                           Yeomen   }
                           Husbandmen   }   Churchwardens
                           Craftsmen   }   Overseers of
                           Tradesmen   }   the Poor

                           Journeymen
                           Apprentices
                           Servants in Husbandry and Industry
1600   Cottagers/Labouring Poor
                           Impotent Poor/Pauper Apprentices
                           Vagrants

Summary – Society: Poverty and the Lower Orders

prosperous yeoman at the beginning of the period, it applied to a much wider range of individuals by 1600. These were the people who became overseers of the poor, churchwardens and parish constables, and held minor administrative posts below the gentry. Earlier, yeomen such as Kett had thought it their duty to represent the grievances of their poorer neighbours. By 1600 the new 'worthies' expected to manage and control the masses. This is seen as undermining neighbourliness and contributing to the social and economic tensions at the end of the century (see page 133).

* Elite attitudes were creating similar social differentiations among the other ranks of the lower orders. Here the division was between being employed or in training and being unemployed and masterless. This set apart the respectable and deserving from the rebellious and undeserving. Such views were ideal stereotypes, but they were very real in the context of late Tudor England and had a considerable impact on an individual's prospects and treatment. Growing numbers of families were living in cottages and overcrowded tenements in the towns and enclosed arable parishes (see page 109). These were the labouring poor, seeking a precarious living from the dual economy (see page 13) and falling into poverty in times of economic slump or harvest failures. They were seen as being basically deserving and respectable. Equally deserving by 1600 were the impotent poor. They were no longer seen as a threat. In return for public relief they were expected to attend church and conform to acceptable standards of behaviour. In marked contrast were the 'able-bodied rogues' who were seen as a threat to the whole fabric of society by being masterless and refusing to work. Only slightly less threatening were those who in increasing numbers were finding work in the expanding industries in the Midlands. The inhabitants of these open parishes were seen as unruly, immoral and ungodly. They, and the vagrant, were the people who the Tudor government sought to reform and discipline.

Making notes on 'Society: Poverty and the Lower Orders'

Refer back to your notes from chapter 5 on general social theories and approaches, and note how interpretations about the lower orders have been revised. Section 2 examines how a peasant society was beginning to change. Make detailed notes on how and why a largely servile medieval peasantry had gained greater independence, but also had become more stratified by 1550. Section 3 examines some aspects of women's history and the family, which are now regarded as highly important in any study of lower order society. You must take care to have a clear grasp of the role of women within and outside the family. You should also note how the family unit influenced social and geographical mobility, especially that of younger children. Section 4 discusses the problem of poverty and vagrancy. Note how interpretations of the causes and nature of poverty have changed. Section 5 examines how the Tudors tried to solve these problems. You need to draw up a very detailed chronological framework of the treatment of poverty and vagrancy. Use the evidence to draw conclusions about the success or failure of the legislation. Section 6 discusses the shape of lower order society in 1600. Note the differences in the social structure in the 1520s, 1550s and 1600.

Answering essay questions on 'Society: Poverty and the Lower Orders'

The Poor Law system – or lack of it – has been an examiners' favourite topic for many years. The issue of how the poor were dealt with by the authorities is therefore worth thinking through in detail. Study the following questions and identify the aspects of the topic that are raised by them. You should come to the conclusion that there are, in fact, only three. What are they? The phrases 'Why were Tudor governments', 'degree of success' and 'effects of' might well feature in your answers.

1. 'Tudor governments found it impossible both to ignore the problem of poverty and to tackle it effectively.' Discuss.
2. How successful were Elizabethan governments in dealing with the social problems that faced them?
3. Examine the view that 'Tudor governments failed to solve the problems of poverty and vagrancy'.
4. Did the poor laws really help the poor in the period up to 1603?
5. Explain the reasons why England had developed a national Poor Law by the end of the sixteenth century.
6. Discuss the judgement that 'the responses of local and national government during the period 1547 to 1603 showed growing awareness of the real reasons for poverty and vagrancy'.

Look at the three 'challenging statement' questions (1, 3 and 6). In each case the examiner is asking you to present a discussion. The safest way to respond to such a request is to describe the ways in which you i) agree and, ii) disagree with the view or views expressed in the quotation. However, your essay would probably receive a higher mark if you were to adopt a more ambitious approach – provided, of course, that you were able to implement it successfully. Examiners often greatly appreciate answers that are based around the differing interpretations of historians; an essay that was mainly made up of a series of 'some historians have argued/claimed this' and 'other historians have argued/claimed that' paragraphs could yield the best results. This is especially so if your conclusion were to explain your point of view and why you hold it.

Source-based questions on 'Society: Poverty and the Lower Orders'

1 The Poor

Carefully read the extracts from London's Guild Hall Journal (1547), given on page 114, and the Act of Parliament (1572), given on page 115, and study the illustration reproduced on page 112. Answer the following questions.

a) Why was it found necessary to pass the ordinance described in the first extract? (*3 marks*)

b) What new element in the funding of poor relief was being introduced in each of the extracts? Why have historians thought that this was a significant change? (*5 marks*)

c) What was the probable effect of this change on the number and size of future charitable donations? Explain your answer. (*3 marks*)

d) What evidence does the illustration provide of the reasons the poor were distrusted and disliked by most of their better-off compatriots? Support your answer by detailed reference to the contents of the illustration. (*7 marks*)

e) In what main ways did prevailing attitudes about the treatment of the poor i) change, and ii) remain constant in Tudor England? (*7 marks*)

CHAPTER 7

Popular Culture

1 Introduction

Since the 1960s, when he published his book *Religion and the Decline of Magic*, K. Thomas has helped to make popular culture an expanding area of study in its own right. Such studies are used as another way of assessing the nature and extent of social change, particularly among the lower orders. An examination of popular culture can reveal a great deal about how people thought and lived together in traditional societies. This is a very useful approach when applied to sixteenth-century England, where a traditional society is thought to have been undergoing change. Three main forces are seen as undermining popular culture – a new elite culture based on humanism and protestantism, commercialisation and the government's wish to enforce law and order through greater centralisation. However, the way in which these forces worked is often very contradictory and the results are difficult to assess. The extent to which a new elite culture was becoming established is very debateable. In any case Elizabethan humanistic culture retained many of the old beliefs. Traditional customs and practices united local communities at village and county levels. This meant that local elites often allied with the lower orders to resist change and protect their own interests, whether the threat came from commercialisation or from government policy. Possibly the greatest dilemma for the authorities was that even those aspects of popular culture which were important in maintaining order and moral discipline within communities were themselves often the cause of riots (see page 128). These issues will be explored in the next two chapters by examining how far popular culture had been undermined and to what extent a new elite culture had emerged by 1600.

Until the fifteenth century the entire laity shared a common culture based on superstition, ritual and fear of the supernatural. As an overwhelming majority of people in all ranks of society were illiterate, this culture was based on oral tradition, with ideas being handed on by word of mouth from generation to generation. Such beliefs were to a large extent endorsed by the medieval Church. The rituals, processions and magic (sacraments and miracles) of the Church were part of the normal life of the people. These ideas were reinforced visually by the carvings of saints and monsters, the stained glass windows and wall paintings in the parish churches. Many of the customs in popular culture reflected the prevailing religious practices and ceremonies. However, other aspects were pre-Christian. Based on ancient legends and myths, they commemorated folk heroes and pagan festivals and were closely linked with traditional farming activities. In popular imagination, alongside the real world of everyday life there existed a spirit world inhabited by ghosts, fairies, vampires and devils. The magic of the Church was seen not only as a means of protection from natural disasters, such as storms and floods, but also against visitations from these supernatural beings. If this failed it was then possible to turn for help to the magicians and sorcerers who were to be found in every town and village. As these beliefs were shared by all ranks of society, they are seen as an accurate reflection of the social attitudes that existed at a given time. Certainly, until the sixteenth century, popular culture was a central part of communal life. Many of the rituals and practices were to protect communities against change and outside interference and helped to unite the local elites and lower orders in a common interest. However, during the sixteenth century economic, religious and cultural changes are considered to have undermined this bond. The outlook of the elites and the lower orders are thought to have begun to diverge, and national interests to have become more important than local loyalties. These are the issues that need to be considered before making any definite judgements about the extent of social change.

The problem is to know how to measure and assess the significance of any cultural changes. Clearly, as medieval popular culture was an oral tradition, it might be considered that it would have been undermined by the growth of lay education in the sixteenth century (see page 137). However, apart from the difficulties of judging the extent of literacy among the laity by 1600, there is evidence to suggest that the spread of literature, such as almanacs, actually strengthened popular culture. Equally, the Renaissance and the Reformation were strong forces encouraging people to think more rationally and, as such, are seen as attacking the irrationality of popular culture. In particular, the spread of Renaissance ideas and humanism in England introduced greater rationality and sophistication among the Tudor elites. This is considered to have begun to separate elite from popular culture. Protestantism, by reducing the superstitions, rituals and magic of the medieval Church, is seen as a major influence against popular culture. On the other hand, it is equally true that by removing the old magical protection of the Church, the Reformation strengthened popular belief in magicians and sorcerers as a means of warding off the supernatural. Similarly, economic developments, such as commercialisation, specialisation and enclosure in agriculture, are thought to have weakened communal loyalties and traditional customs. Yet, alternatively, it can be said that growing discontent, such as ritualistic enclosure riots to protect community rights, actually strengthened popular culture. The evidence is very conflicting and it is difficult to judge to what extent elite and popular culture had become separated by 1603.

2 Traditional Customs

Village life was based on agriculture and the seasons. Work was often leisurely in slack periods, and the year was punctuated by holy days and feast days. This meant that because life in the whole of Western Europe was based largely on agriculture it shared this common culture. However, continental practices were often different from those in England, and every community had its own customs which might vary slightly from its neighbours. The first essential type of community action in the village was co-operation in the farming routine. This was particularly true at busy times of the year such as ploughing, sowing and harvesting. These occupations were carried out to a traditional routine by all the villagers who shared in the essential task of ensuring a good harvest. The harsh routine of life was supported by mutual help. Tools, ploughs and work animals were lent and borrowed. The whole village would combine in the building or repair of houses. Equally, those anti-social enough to allow weeds to flourish or animals to stray or to fail to keep ditches clear were fined and punished. The whole village worked together on the same days and enjoyed their leisure together on feast days, holidays, weddings and wakes with drinking, dancing, games and sports. Alterations in farming practices, such as enclosure and commercialisation, had a strong impact and would, by undermining traditional loyalties, be a cause of social change.

The inhabitants regarded their community as a sacred place which had to be protected against outsiders and strangers. There were various rituals for this purpose which were often associated with the parish church. Every year in Rogation Week the village priest led a procession of all the villagers around the parish boundary. The ceremony of 'beating the bounds' was to reaffirm the 'sacred space' and to familiarise children and newcomers with the topography of the village. The procession was usually accompanied by dancing and the singing of psalms or hymns. It stopped at traditional sites, such as wayside crosses or even ancient burial mounds, and prayers were said for the crops to grow, to placate the weather and to avert natural disasters. As the villagers were very much at the mercy of the weather they had their own rituals, often parodying those of the Church, to deflect hailstorms, snow or floods. The most common form of community ritual to deter outside intrusion into the village and to punish moral transgressions by the inhabitants were 'skimmingtons'. These took the form of processions, accompanied by music and dancing, which were aimed at the offenders (see page 128). Anti-enclosure riots often took the form of a skimmington, and were communal attempts to stop the traditional farming practices being eroded and to protect access to common land.

   * Many intruders were not in human form. In a universe thought to be populated by devils, hobgoblins, vampires, werewolves, fairies, ghosts, witches and magicians it was very important to guard against

the supernatural. Many of these ideas were pre-Christian, while others had slowly accumulated over the centuries. The medieval Church had absorbed much of this mythology. Pagan gods, ancient kings and folk heroes had become associated with Christian saints, while many churches were built on the sites of former pagan temples and sacred enclosures. The rituals, processions and ceremonies of the Church merged in popular imagination into the traditions of folk culture. The power of the medieval Church was itself supernatural. A priest could intercede with God, pray for the crops, exorcise ghosts and drive out devils. Prayers and holy water were seen as the most potent means of combating the devil and the powers of darkness. This meant that the laity regarded the Church as its main defence against supernatural powers and beings. However, the Reformation removed most of this protection. The former rituals were abolished and traditional beliefs were attacked as superstitious myths by the Protestant intellectuals. This left the great mass of the lower orders feeling very exposed to the unknown forces which they still thought ruled their lives.

Even before the Reformation the Church had not been the only means of protection against supernatural forces. In every village and town there were 'cunning' folk who could be consulted in times of adversity. This term was applied equally to sorcerers, magicians and witches, although it was difficult to distinguish good white witches from their evil black counterparts. Such people protected the community and could use their occult powers for a great variety of purposes. For a fee they could heal the sick, find lost property, foretell the future, predict disasters, forecast the weather and counteract spells, curses and bewitchment. In Tudor England such ideas were held by all ranks of society. Indeed, it was important for scholars to be able to show themselves as able magicians and sorcerers. Even radical Protestant reformers endorsed many of these notions. The masses believed themselves to be at the mercy of the whims of fate, and it was difficult to establish the idea that individuals were capable of determining their own destiny. This seems to indicate that, even by 1600, cultural polarisation in Tudor society was not very wide.

On the other hand, there is no doubt that popular culture was under attack by the Tudor authorities, who saw it as a source of disturbance, sedition and insubordination. At the same time, increased secular education and growing rationality led Protestant and Renaissance intellectuals to question the validity of a body of thought based upon traditional superstitions. However, there are doubts about the extent to which the elites had abandoned their belief in many aspects of popular culture by 1600. Although they were beginning to question the existence of fairies and ghosts, the reality of witches and sorcerers was totally accepted. Indeed, Renaissance thought, with its emphasis on neoplatonism (a philosophy based on classical ideas mixed with eastern mysticism), tended to reinforce belief in magic and spirits among the elites. Equally, the Reformation strengthened popular resort to primitive magic by removing the proctective rituals and superstitions of the medieval Church. This meant that, although the Elizabethan government was anxious to remove the disorder, superstition and spreading of rumours associated with popular culture, it made little headway in changing public attitudes.

* Undoubtedly, by the end of the century increasing levels of education were beginning to undermine total acceptance of popular culture throughout society. The more rational Renaissance secular culture, with its belief in man's ability to control natu e (see page 136), was removing the fear of natural disasters among a widening cross-section of the elites. Protestant reformers, especially the Puritans, attacked popular beliefs as superstitious rituals bordering on blasphemy and popery which encouraged moral and sexual laxity. In this they were supported by the government, which saw them as a cause of idleness, insubordination and public disorder. Community collectivism was itself being disrupted. The wealthier villagers and townsmen – the 'worthies' – were beginning to associate themselves with the cultural attitudes of the elites and to distance themselves from the rowdy pastimes and customs of the labouring masses. At the same time community independence was under threat from the growing power and influence of the state, with firmer enforcement of laws governing such things as rioting, vagrancy and poverty. As these changes came at a time when increased migration resulting from enclosure was weakening the effectiveness of communal action, it is not surprising that popular culture was under threat. However, this was a very long-term process which many historians consider was not even complete by the nineteenth century.

3 Community Activities and Action

Before the Reformation much of community life had centred around the Christian calendar and the practices of the medieval Church. This had the effect of uniting the lower orders and the local elites into a common interest. To a large extent the festivals, rituals and processions of the Church merged into those of popular custom. Church practices of blessing the crops while 'beating the bounds' and harvest thanksgiving were shared by the community and mirrored in rituals to drive away hailstorms or divert floods. Much of the communal activity was associated with Church festivals, such as Christmas or Shrove Tuesday, and with holy days and saints' days. Other festivals such as Maytime, mid-summer and New Year, had more pagan connections. However, they were all celebrated by the elites with cavalcades and processions, which were replicated by popular 'ridings', dancing and festivities. Such occasions, being holidays, were an opportunity for games and entertainment to release the stresses of work and harsh conditions. In this respect they were seen by the authorities as a safety-valve, providing that matters did not get out of hand and end in rioting.

This was particularly important because the significance of such events was one of role-reversal. Festivals were seen as times when everyday conventions did not apply. The origin of this notion was the 'lord of misrule' who presided over Christmas celebrations, when order was turned upside down and the lowliest were placed at the top and the mightiest at the bottom. A good example was the custom in the medieval Church of the 'boy bishop', when the youngest choir boy replaced the bishop for a day. (Even today the idea is preserved by the British army, the officers serving the other ranks with Christmas dinner.) For this reason festive events were regarded as a time when the lower orders could mock the authorities and their social superiors. Many popular rituals were parodies of secular and ecclesiastical official procedures. As such they were sometimes used to attack unpopular local landowners or urban authorities. This was particularly true if newcomers, unaware of local customs, had taken over property or assumed office. In many respects the JPs welcomed popular proceedings against people who flouted public opinion, because this augmented the work of the local courts and helped to prevent large-scale disorder. Indeed, there was a long tradition that the people had the right to take action against those who broke local customs if the law officers had failed to remedy the situation. This required a very delicate balance of trust and mutual respect between the local ruling elites and the ruled masses. As long as the lower orders thought that the authorities were being fair and impartial, order and harmony prevailed. However, injustice or failure to act could lead quickly to disorder, such as enclosure riots.

* Communities in Tudor England continued to have a traditional body of beliefs and had similar values and attitudes towards acceptable behaviour. Anyone contravening these standards was publicly humiliated. The normal method used was to organise a 'groaning' or a 'charivari' (also known as a 'skimmington ride'). One of the major causes of such events was sexual immorality, or women becoming over-assertive. Popular tradition was very strongly patriarchal and this was reflected in the desire to ensure the subordination of women. In this respect popular culture closely mirrored intellectual views among the elites (see page 140). However, it is far from clear which of these two attitudes was the cause of growing male dominance in Tudor England. 'Scolds' (nagging women) appear to have been a particular annoyance. It was considered the duty of a husband to keep his wife under control so as to maintain the order and harmony of the community. A woman was expected to be docile, obedient and submissive. In minor cases the wife was punished. A turbulent woman was ducked in the village pond in a 'cucking stool', or forced to wear a 'scold's bridal' over her head with a leather strap across her mouth for a few days. Other lesser

offenders were placed in the stocks, a device in which the arms or legs were locked into a wooden block, to be pelted with stones and rubbish by the children and other passers-by.

If a man proved totally unable to control has wife, or if she was thought to be committing adultery, the husband was punished because he was failing to carry out his social duties. Initially the community expressed its disquiet by gathering around the couple's house and 'groaning', or they played musical instruments, danced, sang bawdy songs and threw rotten vegetables, manure and dead animals through the windows or down the chimney. If the household was considered to be totally out of control a full-scale charivari or skimmington was organised. This took the form of an elaborate procession, or 'riding'. The husband was forced to ride backwards on a horse, donkey or a pole (cowl staff). He was dressed in women's clothes and, in the case of adultery, had to wear animal horns to show that he had been cuckolded. He was led in procession by the other male members of the community dressed in festive costume and often wearing ritualistic animal horns, carrying and firing weapons. The cavalcade was accompanied by music, dancing and songs and verses deriding the husband, who was continuously pelted with rotten vegetables and other filth. These practices are seen as showing the sexual double standard in Tudor England. Adultery and sexual immorality among women were strongly disapproved of and censored by the elites and lower orders alike, while similar behaviour by men was accepted as the norm. Such attitudes may well have been strengthened by commercialisation. As women were becoming increasingly relegated to low paid work (see page 29) their economic contribution to the family was reduced. This is thought to have helped to marginalise women within society.

* Ritualistic demonstrations of this type were a normal part of daily life. They could form part of inter-community rivalry, with groups from one village invading another. Quite frequently members of the local gentry organised and participated in such events as part of their own quarrels with their neighbours. As they normally took place on festivals or holy days, popular demonstrations were regarded as part of the holiday entertainment and provided comic farce to relieve local tensions. People attending festivals who refused to pay contributions to the lord of misrule were often themselves given a mild form of skimmington ride. By 1600 popular action of this nature was still part of the common culture of both the elites and the lower orders, and was by no means condemned by the intellectuals. Although the government was increasingly suspicious, on the grounds that they were a cause of disorder, attracted malcontents and were a threat to property, there was no attempt made to stop the practice.

4 Witchcraft

It was difficult to distinguish between witches and other sorts of cunning people, and in any case there were good and bad (white and black) witches. The main difference appears to have been whether the individual was considered to have been working for good or evil. It was thought that most of the techniques of the cunning people could be practised by anyone who knew the right formula. However, witches could perform their art involuntarily because they possessed personal psychic and occult powers, and it was claimed that witches could kill with just their eyes. During this period English concepts of witchcraft differed from those on the continent where it was claimed that witches were in league with the devil. This idea of the *maleficium* was closely related to heresy and was heightened by religious conflict between Protestants and Catholics. Most witches were thought to be female and this was linked to the supposed sexual excesses of women. On the continent it was claimed that witches' sabbaths involved sexual intercourse with the devil, and that the participants gave birth to diabolical children. The concept of *maleficium* was well known among the Elizabethan intellectuals through continental literature. However, there is no evidence of English witches being accused of diabolical practices until after 1603. Even so, the great majority of people accused of witchcraft in England were women. Generally, they came from the lower orders and were often poor or destitute old women. Their accusers were also frequently women – generally from a higher social level – who claimed that they or their family had been harmed by the 'evil eye'. This has led to the suggestion that accusations of witchcraft in late Tudor England were a sign of a growing rift between the elites and the lower orders and a breakdown in good neighbourly relations. Dislike of the poor and vagrants is thought to have created an irrational fear of the destitute and the travelling stranger, both of whom were often the victims of witchcraft accusations.

* Whether this interpretation is true or not there certainly was an upsurge in witchcraft accusations towards the end of Elizabeth I's reign. Even by 1559 Bishop Jewel was by no means alone in his comment that 'the number of witches and sorcerers had everywhere become enormous'. To what extent the change was a consequence of the Reformation is not clear. Previously witchcraft had been an ecclesiastical offence dealt with in the Church courts. In 1542 witchcraft became a common law crime punishable by hanging, and murder by witchcraft became a separate offence from ordinary murder. The statute was re-enacted in 1563, and in 1581 an act was passed specifically making prophecies and enchantments directed against the monarchy a felony punishable by death.

Act Against Conjurations, Inchantments and Witchraft, 1563

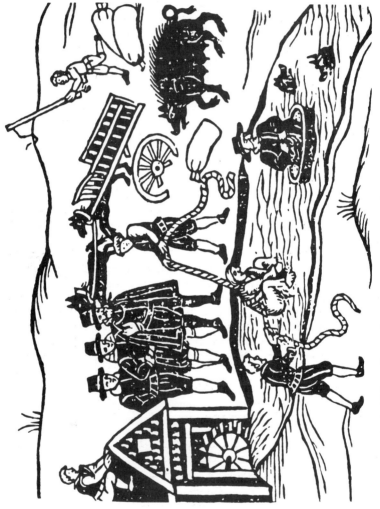

The Swimming of Mary Sutton

1 If any person use, practise, or exercise any invocations or
  conjurations of evil and wicked spirits, to or for any intent or
  purpose; or else if any person or persons . . . use, practise any
  witchcraft, enchantment, charm or sorcery, whereby any person
5 shall happen to be killed or destroyed . . . [they] shall suffer pains
  of death as a felon . . . and if any person shall use, practise, or
  exercise and witchcraft, enchantment, charm or sorcery, whereby
  any person shall happen to be wasted, consumed, or lamed in his
  or her body or whereby any goods or chattels of any person shall
10 be destroyed, wasted, or impaired, then every such offender [will]
  suffer imprisonment for one whole year.

Clearly the possibility of witchcraft was intellectually accepted and was
widely discussed in books, such as Reginald Scot's *Discourse of
Witchcraft*, published in 1584. Indeed, as witches were mentioned in
the bible anyone denying their existence was considered to be an
atheist.

   * The increase in anti-witchcraft legislation has led some historians
to suggest that the fear of witches was provoked by the government,
and was not just a sign of a break-down in social relationships. The
Reformation and the increase in printed books from the continent are
thought to have begun a merger of traditional English ideas with the
newer concepts of diabolical compacts. On the continent witchcraft had
become linked with heresy, while in England it was associated with
popery, sedition and disorder. The passing of statutes making witchcraft a felony enabled the elites to use the courts to prosecute witches
who were seen as enemies of God and the state. Furthermore, it is
considered that Tudor witchcraft legislation was enacted at times of
political instability and was aimed more at preserving public order and
averting the dangers of Catholic plots than against witches. However,
doubts have been cast on the idea that a rising tide of hatred against
witches was initiated by the Elizabethan government and the intellectual elites. It is pointed out that it was not until 1604 that an
anti-witchcraft statute mentioned the idea of diabolical compacts.
Moreover, studies of court cases show that they were mostly brought by
the general public, not by the authorities, and that many JPs were
unwilling to prosecute or convict the accused.

   * Even so, there is no doubt that there was a rising fear of witches in
late Tudor England, although not on the scale of the hysteria later in
the seventeenth century. It has been calculated that in Essex during the
1580s 13 per cent of the criminal cases before the courts concerned
witchcraft accusations brought by members of the public. This has led
many historians to conclude that the attack on witches resulted from
growing traumas within society. It is thought that the rapid pace of
social change created tensions within communities. Indeed, in 1587 an
Essex clergyman suggested that terror of witches sprang from growing

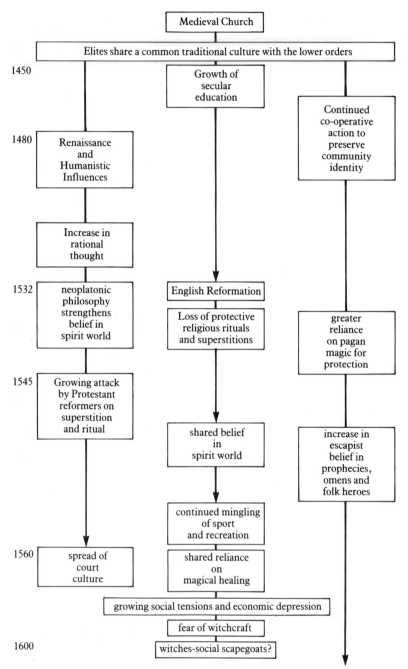

Medieval Church

Elites share a common traditional culture with the lower orders

1450

Growth of secular education

Continued co-operative action to preserve community identity

1480

Renaissance and Humanistic Influences

Increase in rational thought

1532

neoplatonic philosophy strengthens belief in spirit world

English Reformation

Loss of protective religious rituals and superstitions

greater reliance on pagan magic for protection

1545

Growing attack by Protestant reformers on superstition and ritual

shared belief in spirit world

increase in escapist belief in prophecies, omens and folk heroes

continued mingling of sport and recreation

1560

spread of court culture

shared reliance on magical healing

growing social tensions and economic depression

fear of witchcraft

1600

witches-social scapegoats?

Summary – Popular Culture

hostility between neighbours. Demographic increase, rising inflation, enclosures and the commercialisation of agriculture, unemployment, poverty, disease and religious changes are seen as creating stresses within the traditional fabric of society. These forces are considered to have reached a peak in late-Elizabethan England, and their effect was heightened by the economic depression. A major result of this was to lead to a break-down in social relationships. Local communities were coming under pressure. Women, vagrants and strangers were all being regarded with great suspicion. Above all, competition is considered to have been the main reason for the break-down in neighbourliness.

The major thrust behind this theory is that witchcraft was considered anti-social. Such an explanation would account for witches suddenly becoming a problem. At the same time it provides a very useful insight into Tudor social change. The Reformation, by removing the ritual magic of the medieval Church, had left the great mass of people feeling vulnerable to the unknown. This happened just when the forces of social change were creating new rifts in society and breaking down the old relationships. The lower orders resented alterations in their traditional life-style and felt pressurised by attempts by the elites to bring about a reformation of manners. Their situation was being made worse by the emergence of the 'worthies', who now identified with the elites instead of representing the grievances of the masses. This left the lower orders feeling even more exposed. On the other hand, the 'worthies' and elites were conscious of the underlying popular resentment and disorder, which they felt threatened their own position. It is thought significant that the vast majority of witchcraft charges were against lower order women, and were brought by their social superiors drawn particularly from among the 'worthies'. Accusations covered death, disease, maiming and 'possessions' (fits and strokes) apparently caused by witchcraft to people and animals, as well as loss and damage to property. Indeed, illness, fires, accidents or anything unexpected and unexplainable could be attributed to witchcraft, malice and the 'evil eye'. Rising social tensions turned witches into the scapegoats of society.

Making notes on 'Popular Culture'

The study of popular culture reveals a great deal about how people and communities lived and thought in Tudor England. Popular culture is difficult to define; use Section 1 to note down all its main elements and the role it and the pre-Reformation Church played in the life of the community. The Reformation was a major cause of cultural change, and so make careful notes about the influence of protestantism and other developments, such as the Renaissance and greater literacy. Use Section 2 to gain a firm grasp of the place of traditional customs within communities. From Section 3 note how rituals and demonstrations were used within communities and consider what this reveals about social attitudes. Section 3 examines the increasing fear of witchcraft in Tudor society. Note the characteristics of witches and the measures taken against them. There are various explanations of the rising fear of witches in late Tudor England. Consider the interpretations and decide what they tell you about the state of society in 1600.

Source-based questions on 'Popular Culture'

1 Witchcraft
Carefully read the extract from the Act of 1563 given on page 129 and study the illustration of 'The Swimming of Mary Sutton' on page 130. Answer the following questions.
a) What two crimes is the Act legislating against? *(2 marks)*
b) In what ways was the Act open to abuse? *(4 marks)*
c) What evidence does the extract provide of mid-Tudor beliefs about witchcraft? *(4 marks)*
d) What other evidence is there that the elites of the time believed in witchcraft and sorcery? *(5 marks)*
e) What is happening to Mary Sutton in the illustration? Why? Explain what the outcomes of the 'swimming' could have been. *(5 marks)*
f) What is the probable significance of i) the cart and what is happening to it, and ii) the sows in the illustration? *(5 marks)*

CHAPTER 8

A New Elite Culture?

1 Introduction

There is considerable debate among historians as to the nature and extent of elite cultural change in Tudor England. There is no disagreement that by 1600 a secular culture based on humanistic and Renaissance thought was well established at the court in London and in many of the larger country houses. What is less certain is the extent to which this new rational and scientific thinking had penetrated into the countryside away from the south-east. It is equally questionable how far these new ideas had replaced the old culture of beliefs that had been common to all ranks of society. The basis of the change in outlook among the elites was the growth in education and literacy that had begun in the late fifteenth century. This was enhanced by the Reformation after 1540 and has been described as an educational revolution. As such opportunities were much greater for the elites, their members are seen as adopting an increasingly literate culture and moving away from the traditional oral beliefs of the lower orders (see page 122). At the same time the rapid growth in legal training and greater emphasis on private property is seen as further undermining popular culture which was based on common rights and community action (see page 126). Another development aiding this process was the further erosion of aristocratic French and ecclesiastical Latin by vernacular English, except for some administrative uses. Although it had been the norm for members of the elites to be bilingual, English had come into general use during the fifteenth century for conversation, literature and business. This growing usage in society brought about a standardisation of English among the elites and so further weakened their local loyalties. Such changes are seen as creating a more rational, refined elite culture which was very different from the boisterous, ritualistic beliefs that it was beginning to replace.

  * However, although much has been written about the flowering of Renaissance culture in Tudor England, the scale of its development and spread by 1600 should not be over-estimated. It has been seen as creating an ever-widening gulf between the educated elites and the illiterate lower orders, but it is important to remember that there are now increasing doubts about how far this polarisation had progressed even by the eighteenth century. Cultural differentiation is a very slow process and it is uncertain that much change had occurred by 1600. The overwhelming majority of people in Tudor England shared a common perception of their surroundings. They had a view of a universe in which the forces of good and evil fought for supremacy, in which their

world was governed by magic and the supernatural. Renaissance intellectuals had begun to think that it was possible for mankind to create harmony and correct the disorder to be found in nature. However, in an unscientific age, the universe was generally regarded as mystical and mysterious. Everyone, from the courtier to the simplest villager, believed in fairies and hobgoblins. Elizabeth I, although she could translate Boethius into English from Greek, feared witches (see page 129) and enjoyed maypole dancing. Gentlemen who could compose elegant sonnets might equally well organise village sports and football matches. It is true that in Elizabethan court circles the bucolic country squire was beginning to be mocked as an unrefined bumpkin, but support for this perception outside London was limited. Although by 1600 urban culture was becoming more sophisticated, it is thought that the elites and lower orders in the countryside largely continued to share a common culture. A major difference was that Renaissance thought and education had begun to give the literate elites a growing confidence that they could control the natural world. The illiterate masses still felt that they were completely at the mercy of the unknown.

* It was this feeling of elite superiority that helped to make a more secular culture. While the Tudor elites continued to believe in heaven and hell and the need to attend church, for them much of the mystery had been taken away from religion. Most of the ritual and symbolism had been removed from Anglican services, and the Church itself was subordinated to the state. The clergy were no longer regarded as the only intermediaries between God and man. The English bible was available for all the laity to read. As education ceased to be the prerogative of the clergy, they came to hold a less prominent role within society. Above all, it was no longer believed that man's only duty on earth was to worship God and prepare for the after-life. Such 'other worldliness' had been replaced by a sharper rationality in which individualism and competition took the place of a passive acceptance of one's pre-ordained position in life. The world was not seen simply as a perfect God-given gift that should not be changed, but as something to be exploited and improved for the benefit of mankind. Such views can be seen in the making of pleasure gardens designed to improve upon nature. Equally, enclosure came to be seen as producing order out of the natural chaos (see page 137).

* These new elite attitudes were reflected in all aspects of life. Although the concept of the 'great chain of being' continued to be held, it came to be seen as a means of social control to uphold the status quo and maintain elite superiority (see page 83). The life-style of polite society was designed to differentiate it from the masses and their social inferiors. The sumptuary laws (see page 84) attempted to define the genteel by their form of dress. Wealth enabled the elites to adopt a luxurious and free-spending existence which came to be regarded as the essential mark of gentility. During the second half of the century the

'great rebuilding' saw the move towards greater material comfort and privacy among the rural and urban elites. Inconvenient castles and barn-like halls were replaced by palaces and country houses, with many reception rooms and bedrooms and equipped with fireplaces and glazed windows. The residences of the elites were provided with tables and chairs, carpets and wall-hangings, and furnished with paintings, gold, silver and other luxuries.

Francis Bacon, Observations on a Libel, 1592

1   There was never the like number of fair and stately houses as have been built and set up from the ground since her Majesty's reign; insomuch that there have been reckoned in one shire that is not great to the number of three and thirty, which have been all
5 new built within that time; and whereof the meanest was never built for two thousand pounds.

    There was never the like pleasures of goodly gardens and orchards, walks, pools and parks, as do adorn almost every mansion house.

10   There was never the like number of beautiful and costly tombs and monuments, which are erected in sundry churches in honourable memory of the dead.

    There was never the like quantity of plate, jewels, sumptuous movables and stuff, as is now within the realm.

15   There was never the like quantity of waste and unprofitable ground inned, [enclosed] reclaimed and improved.

Apart from living in the right setting, a gentleman had to behave in the correct manner. Humanistic thought, while recognising the need for a lavish life-style, placed great stress on moderation and the need to avoid excess. A gentlemen had to be well educated, speak foreign languages and travel widely at home and abroad. He had to be proficient in all the skills, such as warfare, riding, hunting, sports, dancing, singing, playing a musical instrument and appreciating art, which were thought to be the mark of gentility. However, it was essential that a gentleman should not become too expert in any of these pursuits. If this happened he was in danger of being thought a professional, or an artisan, which would mean loss of social status.

2 Education and Literacy

Education is seen as a major force in bringing about the eventual separation of elite and popular culture. Greater levels of literacy created a more sophisticated and rational elite society which became increasingly sceptical about many of the traditional ideas and customs of the lower orders. There was also a growth of literacy among the middle ranks of

society. This, it is thought, accelerated the process of social stratification because the new 'worthies' associated with the elites and looked
down on the masses. At the same time, the patriarchal view of society,
held by both the elites and lower orders, was strengthened because even
elite women became more marginalised by their lack of educational
opportunities.

There is abundant evidence to support the suggestion that lay literacy
was increasing rapidly from the end of the fifteenth century. This
process was helped by the development of printing which, by replacing
the slow and expensive process of writing manuscripts by hand, made
books much cheaper and much more available. Moreover, much of this
literature was being written in English instead of Latin or French. Wills
and inventories show that many of the urban and rural elites possessed
books and sometimes libraries before 1500. These often contained a
variety of reading material: bibles, devotional books, histories, philosophy, romances and copies of Chaucer, as well as books on warfare,
chess, coats of arms and chivalry in a number of languages. Women also
frequently left books to their relatives, and it appears that female
literacy was quite high at this time. A reason for this was that many
daughters of the elites were boarded at nunneries to be educated, even
if it was not intended that they should enter the Church (see page 87).
Schools for boys were still largely organised and staffed by clergy and
monks. Cathedrals and monasteries all had schools attached to them, as
did many parish churches. Most of these were choir or song schools,
with a schoolmaster to give the young boys basic tuition. The more
gifted were then given a more formal education in grammar (including
Latin) before going to university.

Alongside such provision there was an increase in lay, secular
schooling. This took several forms. A great majority of the children of
the elites were still trained in large households (see page 88). However,
during the fifteenth century this practical education was being sup-
plemented by the provision of schoolmasters to teach literacy and some
grammar. At the same time many new schools were being established.
The largest examples were Eton and Winchester which provided
secondary grammar education for the sons of the elites. Most new
schools were much smaller and were created by lay benefactors in towns
and villages all over the country. A large number were associated with
chantries, where the founder left money for a priest to sing masses for
his soul and those of his family and to teach local children. Others were
associated with religious guilds, and some were linked to bequests left
for the upkeep of roads and bridges, or donations to the poor. In
general such schools provided 'petty' (elementary) education for younger children, although some taught grammar as well. Many of these
schools differed from their Church counterparts in that the curriculum
was not theological. Often the benefactor specified that subjects such as
accountancy, mathematics, book-keeping and estate management

should be taught. A large number were free and provided education for all ranks of society of both sexes.

* The Reformation brought a further rapid expansion in secular education. Already by 1500 humanistic thought was stressing the need for a wider education, bible reading and an interest in the classics for men. These ideals were fostered by schools, such as St Paul's, established by John Colet in London. The Protestant reformers also stressed the need for wider (male) education and literacy. However, the initial impact of the Reformation was to sweep away a great number of the existing schools. The dissolution of the monasteries and chantries brought the closure of the attached schools and those run by religious guilds and charitable foundations. Although the government stipulated that the income from such confiscated lands should be used for the benefit of the local community by providing hospitals, almshouses and schools, large amounts were seized by the royal commissioners or passed into lay hands. As in the case of the almshouses and hospitals (see page 108), it was left to private benefactors and local authorities to re-establish the education system. Two main types of school became widely distributed across the country: the petty schools for young children to learn reading and writing in English, and the grammar schools where children up to the age of 16 were taught mainly grammar, Latin, Greek and the classics. It is virtually impossible to calculate the number of schools established by 1600. Some still exist, others have disappeared, many were not open continuously, depending on the availability of a schoolmaster, or were not officially recorded. In Cambridgeshire it has been estimated that there were well-established schools in 23 of the smaller towns and villages, and possibly some form of schooling in up to 50 other villages. Some of the schools were free, while a sliding scale of fees were charged in others. Such provision meant that some form of education was widely available for the elites and lesser elites in both town and country, and probably to those much further down the social ranks as well.

* The establishment of numerous schools shows the growing import-ance placed on literacy in English. Equally the classical curriculum of the grammar school indicates the strength of humanistic thought. Emulating genteel culture education was rapidly becoming a necessity for the elites and the growing numbers of emerging worthies. In an increasingly competitive society, literacy and some knowledge of the law was a basic need for survival. This meant that even eldest sons who would inherit an estate, farm or business needed to be educated so that they could protect their interests. For younger sons education was possibly even more important because without it they stood little chance of advancing their careers. At the same time it was becoming accepted that education was the mark of gentility, so that anyone aspiring to elite status had to be well schooled.

With the growing humanistic stress on education and refinement of manners, the old military training became less popular. Knighthood became associated with civil duties and Elizabeth I disapproved of soldiers being knighted for bravery on the field of battle. Partly for this reason, the practice of sending sons to be trained in large households at the age of seven, which had been common among the gentry, was replaced by schooling up to the age of 16. The nobility continued to have their sons trained at court or in each other's households, but even here formal teaching was playing a much more central role. Education for girls was regarded as less essential, partly because the importance attached to men in Renaissance thinking reinforced the already highly patriarchal nature of society (see page 127). At the same time the closure of the nunneries had removed one of the important openings for female education. This meant that most elite girls continued to be trained in household management and the accomplishments, such as dancing, singing, embroidery and the playing of musical instruments, thought necessary to make a successful marriage and to be a credit to their husband. Although girls from the lesser elites were allowed to attend some schools, many were being restricted to boys only.

Higher education at the universities or the Inns of Court had become almost essential for boys from the elites. The universities were less favoured by the nobility and gentry as a possible route to theological training because preferment in the Church had become unfashionable with the decline in the status of the clergy. However, many of the sons of the lesser elites still found this a valuable career route. Moreover, many gentry sons attended university, even if they did not stay long enough to graduate, because it was considered that this would give them extra polish. To cater for this, Oxford and Cambridge provided ample private tuition in such things as fencing, dancing and languages. For these reasons there was a great expansion in the number of students between 1560 and the 1580s. Many went directly to the Inns of Court, or after a few terms at university. Not only was the value of legal training recognised, but residence in the capital gave the opportunity to attend the royal court and obtain patronage. Equally, it was a chance to experience the low-life of London. After completing their studies, many took up careers but some stayed on at court or in a noble household. Others travelled abroad to complete their education. Like all such travellers, they were expected to keep diaries and send letters and drawings describing what they saw (especially castles and fortifications) to the privy council, because this was regarded as potentially useful military information.

3 Architecture and Lifestyle

An outward sign of the polarisation in Tudor society and culture was the growing sophistication and comfort of the houses of the nobility and the gentry and, on a smaller scale, those of the urban and lesser rural elites. By 1600 there was a sharp distinction between the houses of the affluent sections of society, and the overcrowded, ramshackle cottages of the labouring poor. Lifestyle had become a hallmark of status and anyone with pretensions of being considered a member of the elites had to emulate the setting and living standards of polite society.

During the sixteenth century lay patronage of building moved away from churches to domestic houses, apart from the popularity of elaborate family memorials (see page 137). The great expansion in Tudor building came at a time of increasing affluence among the elites, and a growing awareness of the importance of appearances as a mark of status. It was also a sign of the greater comparative peace in England, which made it possible to move out of inconvenient castles and damp, moated manor houses. At the same time it gave the elites the opportunity for greater privacy and comfort. At the end of the middle ages the hall was the central feature of all houses from the great house down to the simplest peasant cottage, with the larger houses having rooms added on haphazardly around the hall. A major feature of Tudor building was the diversification of living and bed rooms in the houses of the upper and middle ranks of society. This was true even when buildings were only modified by dividing up the hall and putting up ceilings to create new second floor rooms. Most of the re-building took place in the countryside, although the urban elites modified and refurnished their houses for display and comfort.

Although the elites were very conscious of Renaissance classical architecture, it had comparatively little influence on the main fabric of buildings before 1600. The main impact was on interior and exterior decoration and in greater symmetry in overall design. Most Tudor building, certainly up to the 1550s, was more gothic (medieval) than classical. Nevertheless, English architecture was influenced by the continental Renaissance, particularly from France and the Netherlands and, to a lesser extent, Italy. However, no distinctive Tudor classical style was created. Most building was very individualistic, and reflected the taste of the owner. During the first half of the century some use was made of continental craftsmen, but most of them are considered to have been very second-rate. It was only during Elizabeth I's reign that English craftsmen began to adopt the new styles and skills. At first their workmanship was clumsy and crude, and it was not until after 1600 that really good quality work was produced. In most elite houses the great hall remained a central feature. The major change was that a much more regular plan was adopted and houses were designed as a whole, not just added to in a piecemeal fashion. This produced the two characteristic 'H' and 'E' plans. In the first the hall formed the crossbar with rooms added at either end. Alternatively the hall formed half of the long stroke of the E. Palaces and very large houses were built round a central court, or courts, in a variety of plans. The large houses were generally built of local stone or brick, as were those of the lesser gentry

Hampton Court Palace

Nonsuch Palace

Longleat

Montacute House

and yeomen. In areas where there was no stone, smaller houses were half-timbered, with the wooden frame filled with brick or lath and plaster. Many of these have survived and are now the characteristic country cottage. The housing of the lower orders was much less durable and normally had to be rebuilt every 10 years.

* The development of Tudor architecture fell into four main phases. During the first half of the century the main patrons were the royal family and officers of state. One of the first major building works was Hampton Court (apart from Greenwich, which was built by Henry VII in a similar style), begun in 1514 by Thomas Wolsey and completed by Henry VIII in 1540 (see page 142). The palace, with its battlements and gothic windows, was almost totally medieval in design and construction. Italian craftsmen were employed to add terracotta classical decoration and heads of Roman emperors to the exterior. Similarly, inside stucco work was used on some of the ceilings, and the timber roof of the great hall had additional Italian decoration. However, classical embellishment was not widely popular in England until the 1540s.

Between the 1520s and the 1560s the main influence was from France and Flanders, although Holbein designed some highly decorated classical fireplaces. The prime example of the Franco-Flemish connection was Nonsuch Palace, started by Henry VIII in 1538 and completed in 1558 at a cost of up to £20,000 a year. As the name suggests, it was to be the most sumptuous building in England. This palace is regarded as an architectural oddity (see page 142), which reflected the king's love of display. On state occasions and pageants highly lavish and flamboyant temporary buildings were erected. Nonsuch is considered to represent this bizarre style, rather than any serious architectural development. Built in stone and plaster framed in wood, the exterior was partly gilded and decorated with plaster strap-work panels depicting pseudo-classical reliefs. It was topped by a great variety of gables, chimneys and battlemented or domed towers. A number of Italian, French and Flemish craftsmen worked on the site and introduced many of the new decorative forms. In particular the widespread use of interior and exterior plaster reliefs was adopted by many English craftsmen, especially for interiors.

Up to this point the only classical influence had been the embellishment of traditional building. From the 1550s French influence appears to have led to a greater use of a Renaissance sense of order and balance in architecture, although many gothic features continued to be incorporated. The Protector Somerset sent John Shute to Italy in 1550 to study Renaissance buildings and his book, *First Chief Grounds of Architecture*, was published in 1563. Somerset himself appears to have incorporated a number of new French features into Somerset House in London, which was built in 1549 but was later destroyed. These included classical columns, balanced window pediments and balustrades. Some of these features were included in other houses built at this time, such as Burghley House in Northamptonshire. The finest examples of complete houses in this new style were Theobalds and Longleat. Theobalds, built in red brick in Hertfordshire by William Cecil, was supposed to be the finest house in England, but it was destroyed and little is known about it. Longleat (see page 143) in Wiltshire was built by Sir John Thynne between 1568 and 1580. He used two builder-architects, Robert Smythson and William Spicer. The plan was still of a medieval courtyard house, but it was symmetrically conceived with flamboyant classical details. The windows were balanced in the Renaissance style and set-off with classical pilasters (columns). The interior was lavishly decorated with plaster work. Smythson also built Wollaton Hall in Nottinghamshire, which is another good example of this style of building.

Elizabeth I was too insecure financially to indulge in lavish building, and it was left to the county elites to develop architecture. There was a tremendous variety of design, as no architects as such yet existed. Each individual employed a builder and either supervised the construction personally, or hired a master of works. Design and decoration were chosen from the many pattern books which were becoming widely available. The lavishness depended upon the wealth of the family. For example, the courtier Sir Henry Poole built Sapperton in Gloucestershire in the style of his relative, Sir John Thynne's, house at Longleat. It had banqueting houses on the roof and in the garden where guests could withdraw after a meal to drink wine and eat sweet-meats while enjoying the views or the gardens. The house was surrounded by Italian and French raised and terraced gardens, a walled kitchen garden, lawns, alleys, arbours, parkland and pasture, all of which were an essential part of the setting. On the other hand, Sir Henry's son-in-law, Sir Richard Fettiplace, could only afford to add a porch and a new fireplace to his twelfth-century moated manor house in Berkshire, and to have the hall divided and ceilinged-over to provide second floor rooms. A typical example of Elizabethan architecture is Montacute House in Somerset (see page 143). Built between 1588 and 1601, it has all the Renaisance features of mouldings, Flemish gables, columnar chimneys and balustrading that were to become common in the seventeenth century.

* It is possible to gain some impression of the lavish splendour of Tudor great houses from the diary of Baron Waldstein, a young German student who visited England in the summer of 1600 and was presented to Elizabeth I.

The Diary of Baron Waldstein, 1600
1 [Hampton Court]
   This is considered to be the most splendid of the palaces and to be
   the best for its collection of tapestries . . . On the gateway are

busts of Trajan and Hadrian . . . Next we went into the garden.
5 This is specially interesting because of its many avenues and also
for the large number of growing plants shaped into animals, in
fact they even had sirens, centaurs, sphinxes, and other fabulous
poetic creatures . . . We went into one room decorated with very
large and choice tapestries showing the story of Julius Caesar and
10 Pompey . . . [In] the Presence Chamber one can see fabulously
rich hangings, in another the sumptuous beds such as Henry
VIII's, which is most gorgeously decorated with gold . . . [In
another] a jewelled water clock . . . a chess set made of alabaster,
the ivory flutes used by the Queens's musicians . . .

15 [Nonsuch]
This is a place of such splendours that it overshadows the glory of
all other buildings far and wide . . . The royal possessions all
about you are so inspired, there are so many miracles of perfected
art [that it fully deserves the name Nonsuch]. Starting in the hall,
20 there is a collection of sculptures representing stories from Ovid
. . . There is also a stonework table with four containers: they run
with wines, beer and water when the Queen is present. After
seeing this we went down into the garden which is the finest in the
whole of England . . . There are three distinct parts: the Grove,
25 the Woodland, and the Wilderness . . .

[Theobalds]
Both the architecture and the furnishings of this great house are
magnificent, and in addition it is notable for the number of its
turrets and for its unrivalled fireplaces . . . In the first room there
30 is an overhanging rock or crag . . . made of different kinds of
semi-transparent stone [a grotto] . . . and inside can be seen a
man and a woman dressed like the wildmen of the woods . . .
There is a room [in which] one bed has its coverlet woven in gold,
another is made of ostrich feathers . . . There is a draughts board
35 with all the pieces made of gold and silver, an oil lamp made of
gold . . .

This is the style of lavish ostentation that the elites aimed to emulate
in their houses. Inventories show that even quite modest households
had an impressive collection of clothes, bedding, wall hangings, silver
and pewter plate, books, jewellery, pictures and ornaments, and had
numerous indoor servants. These were all necessary to show the status
of anyone aspiring to the elites. Many of these embellishments might be
stored away for much of the year, but they were all brought out for
display when the family entertained. Although hospitality was thought
to be declining (see page 108), it was still on a vast scale. If Elizabeth I
visited one of the nobility in the course of one of her 'progresses' around

Juno, Pallas Athene and Venus, together with Queen Elizabeth

the country, she and the entire court would have to be entertained for several days. Smaller households would be expected to cater for 100 guests on important festivals, and even an intimate family party would be attended by up to 40 people. Such gatherings might be prolonged. For many families Christmas and New Year celebrations began in November and lasted into February. While the vast scale of medieval banquets was becoming unfashionable, it was thought that three courses, each consisting of 32 dishes, were essential for a quite modest meal. While many of the dishes were vegetables, custards, tarts and pastries, a substantial proportion were large meat pies, together with chicken, beef, venison, swan and other game. The table had to be set out in a formal pattern resembling a knot garden (see page 88) and each dish had to be removed and replaced with another so as not to break up the design.

It was highly important for elite wives to be good household managers. Many appear to have been very literate and to have compiled house and recipe books. Elinor Poole, the eldest daughter of Sir Henry Poole, who married Sir Richard Fettiplace of Appleton (see page 145) in 1589, kept such a book. In it are several hundred recipes for a great variety of dishes, jams and cordials, as well as for medicines, poultices and other cures. These were collected from relatives and her very wide circle of friends. For example, Sir Walter Raleigh contributed a recipe for tobacco cordial. Not only did elite wives have to oversee the elaborate preparations for meals, but they were also expected to arrange the entertainments that went with them. Tables would be decorated with such things as plasterboard castles and ships, which would exchange fire with miniature cannons during the meal; or pastry stags filled with wine which ran all over the table when it was shot with arrows; or large pies filled with live birds and frogs. Recreations, such as music, dancing, masques and games, had to be arranged each evening, as well as hunting and other sports during the day.

4 Courtly Graces

The houses, furnishings and gardens of the elites were designed to set them apart from the common masses. Equally, as manners and behaviour were seen as a sign of social superiority, great attention was paid to etiquette by polite society. Lifestyle was becoming governed by the Renaissance concept that moderation and sophistication were the essence of gentility.

Elite attitudes towards the arts, literature and music were governed by the humanistic ideals of elegance and moderation. In cultural terms, a gentleman had to excel at all things, but in an easy, casual manner. Such attitudes owed much to Italian influence. Many books were written, or translated from Italian, such as Thomas Hoby's *The*

Courtyer published in 1561, detailing the etiquette of genteel society. Elite women were equally expected to be proficient in all things suited to their station in life. They had to be skilled in playing musical instruments, dancing and singing, but in a manner designed to show off the greater accomplishmeents of their male partners. Mastery of all such skills was thought to separate the elites from their social inferiors. However, there was a sharp debate with both Puritans and moralists who saw the new code of manners as lax, wanton and showing a marked decline from earlier standards of behaviour. These attitudes are well illustrated by two books on dancing. In 1531 Sir Thomas Elyot considered that men and women dancing together expressed the 'figure of very nobility', because it combined man, who 'in his natural perfection is fierce, hardy, strong in opinion, covetous of glory, desirous of knowledge', with woman, who by nature is 'mild, timorous, tractable, gentle, decorous, faithful'. On the other hand, John North-brooke, writing in 1579, considered dancing to have been invented by the 'devils of hell', because men and women 'dance to wanton songs and dishonest verses' and 'maidens and matrons are groped and handled by unchaste hands, and kissed and dishonestly embraced'.

* By the reign of Elizabeth I the Renaissance gentleman was expected to dabble in all the refinements of leisure. At the same time he was expected to be a patron of art and to give employment to professional artists, writers and craftsmen. As was the case in so many aspects of Tudor England, reliance on continental expertise in these areas was only just beginning to be replaced by native skills by 1600. Throughout the sixteenth century the court at Westminster was the major centre of patronage, although there was a steady increase in the sophistication of the country houses, especially in the south.

Some proficiency in, and appreciation of, the visual arts was a necessary gentlemanly accomplishment. In Renaissance thought poetry and painting were linked together. Gentlemen were expected to be knowledgeable about the merits of works of art and classical statuary. All the great houses had their collections of paintings and galleries in which to display classical statues bought through agents or collected during travels abroad. Many of the painting commissioned by the elites were allegories based on classic themes. Likewise much of Elizabethan poetry, literature and drama had a similar basis, which linked the various art forms together. For example a painting *Juno, Pallas Athene, and Venus, together with Queen Elizabeth* (see page 147), of 1569, shows the queen winning the prize of beauty. Such allegory becomes linked with Edmund Spencer's epic poem *The Fairie Queen*, and together they formed the core of the cult of 'Gloriana', in praise of Elizabeth as the 'virgin queen', which superseded the religious cult of the Virgin Mary. This became a favourite theme of the Elizabethan court pageant and festivities. Military contest in tournaments was replaced by chivalric pageantry, where courtiers fought mock battles to win the castle of

Love, Honour or Albion in which was seated the queen and her ladies in waiting. Similar themes formed the subject of elaborate court dramatic productions, or masques, where the queen and her courtiers played the principal roles in classical or allegorical stories, in which harmony was often opposed to the disorder of the world and which were set to music, verse and dance.

5 Conclusion

Historians find it difficult to decide to what extent a new elite culture had become established by 1600. Certainly Elizabethan literature of all kinds suggests that a reformation of manners was creating a more refined elite society which was distancing itself from the disorderly and vulgar lower orders. The fact that so many books were being written to support or condemn the behaviour and attitudes of the Elizabethan elites seems to support the idea that a new culture was emerging. Puritans and moralists bemoaned the loss of traditional values and criticised the laxity of manners. Humanists, while praising new enlightened thinking and refinement, warned against excess. Many of the elites praised the countryside as being the haven of honest values, hospitality and manly sports, as opposed to London and the court which were seen as artificial and decadent. Others maintained that a gentleman needed to acquire the grace and elegance that could be obtained only in the city and through travel.

    * When Elizabeth I died, English society and economy showed great contrasts and diversity. Opulent wealth existed alongside grinding poverty, and magnificent palaces stood among ruinous tenements and slums. Vast fortunes were being made while the harvest failures and economic recession of the 1590s had brought unemployment, near starvation and destitution to large sections of the labouring poor. Life was very much a wheel of fortune, with large numbers of younger children from all sections of society trying to establish themselves. Violence and disorder were countered by harsh laws and brutal punishments. Elizabethan society was very much in transition. Significant changes were taking place, but within a context of considerable underlying continuity. London and the other towns were beginning to exert a growing influence on the countryside, but England was still overwhelmingly rural. Although government attempts to impose greater uniformity and centralisation were succeeding, county societies retained much independence. In 1603 England was a country of great diversity where traditional localism remained dominant.

    Even so, historians are doubtful about the extent to which new cultural ideas had spread outside London, the court and the great country houses by 1600. Many of the elites were still illiterate, and so would have had little knowledge of the new ideas. Penetration into the traditional county communities appears to have been limited. Certainly

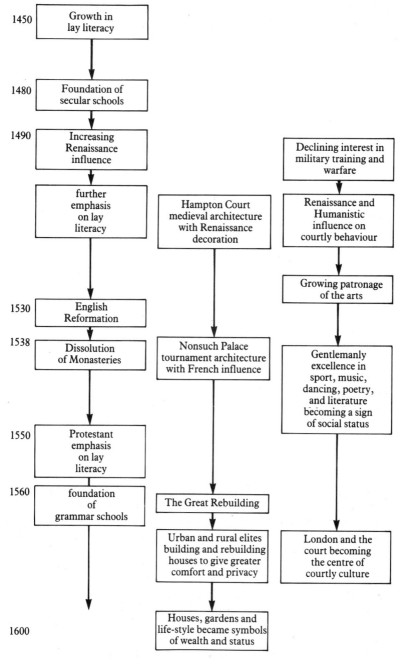

Summary – A New Elite Culture?

the elites, and even the courtiers, continued to participate in rural seasonal festivities and games. All sections of society still believed in magic and witchcraft. Although an elite culture had begun to develop, the degree of separation from popular beliefs seems to have been slight by 1600. Under a thin veneer of refinement, Elizabethan polite society was still violent and superstitious.

Making notes on 'A New Elite Culture'

You need to know what forces are thought to have changed elite culture between 1450 and 1600. Use Section 1 to note the extent such influences as education, the Renaissance and the Reformation had in creating new elite attitudes. Section 2 examines changes in education. Note the way in which education and attitudes towards literacy and learning developed during the period. From Section 3 make detailed notes on the way in which Tudor architecture developed, and how attitudes towards comfort, privacy and lifestyle were changing. Compare the arguments for and against the emergence of a new elite culture by 1600. To help you decide the extent of any changes, refer back to your notes on chapter 7 and consider how far elite culture had diverged from popular culture. Finally, refer back to your notes on chapters 5 and 6 and identify the ways in which the discussion on cultural developments has helped you to estimate the extent of change in Tudor society.

Source-based questions on 'A New Elite Culture?'

1 Conspicuous Expenditure
Carefully read the extracts from Francis Bacon's *Observation on a Libel*, given on page 137, and Baron Waldstein's diary, given on pages 145 and 146, and study the illustrations of Hampton Court, Nonsuch Palace, Longleat and Montacute House reproduced on pages 142 and 143. Answer the following questions.
a) Was Bacon supportive of or hostile to the expenditure he described? Substantiate your answer with at least two phrases quoted from the extract. *(3 marks)*
b) What, in general terms, so impressed Baron Waldstein about Hampton Court, Nonsuch and Theobolds? *(3 marks)*
c) Examine the illustrations of Hampton Court and Nonsuch. What aspects of the buildings (in general and specific terms) as illustrated

are likely to have impressed Baron Waldstein? Justify your answer. (*6 marks*)

d) Examine the illustrations of Longleat and Montacute. Explain the ways in which the two buildings typify the polite architecture of late sixteenth century England. (*5 marks*)

e) Why was the expenditure described in the extracts so much more conspicuous in Elizabeth's reign than earlier in the century? (*4 marks*)

f) What have historians considered to have been the effects on the English economy of the large-scale spending by the elites on their houses and contents? (*4 marks*)

2 Art and Elite Culture

Study the painting 'Juno, Pallas Athene, and Venus, together with Queen Elizabeth' reproduced on page 147 and the detail of the painting 'Portrait of Sir Henry Unton' reproduced on the front cover. Answer the following questions.

a) Describe what is happening in the illustration on the front cover. (*3 marks*)

b) The front cover illustration is a detail from a large picture depicting scenes from the life of Sir Henry Unton, an Elizabethan gentleman. What message is the artist attempting to give the viewer by including this scene in his painting? Explain your answer. (*5 marks*)

c) What message is the artist of 'Juno, Pallas Athene, and Venus, together with Queen Elizabeth' attempting to communicate? Explain your answer. (*6 marks*)

d) In what ways do the two pictures differ in terms of their accessibility to the viewer? What does this suggest about the state of elite culture in late Elizabethan England? (*6 marks*)

Further Reading

The amount written about Tudor society and economy increases every year as new approaches and interpretations are adopted. The books range from general histories through to specialist secondary studies on every aspect of Tudor England. You should read general histories to obtain a sound over-view, and, although your time is limited, use some of the more specialist works to gain an understanding of the historical debate over the complexities of the period. There follows a short selection of the more available and readable examples of this type of material.

J. Youings, *Sixteenth Century England* (Penguin Books, 1984)

This is the most recent book giving a comprehensive coverage of Tudor society. It contains a great variety of examples drawn from contemporary writings, and has a full and informative bibliography.

W.G. Hoskins, *The Age of Plunder, King Henry's England 1500–1547* (Longman, 1976)

D.M. Palliser, *The Age of Elizabeth, England Under the Later Tudors 1547–1603* (Longman, 1983)

These two books offer contrasting approaches to Tudor society.

D.C. Coleman, *The Economy of England 1450–1750* (OUP, 1977)

This is still the most comprehensive and uncomplicated general account of the English economy, and covers the essential period of the 'long sixteenth century' from 1450 to 1650. In addition it has many useful graphs and tables.

P. Slack, *Poverty and Policy in Tudor and Stuart England* (Longman, 1987)

This is probably the fullest and most recent book about poverty in Tudor England.

I. Wallerstein, *The Modern World – System 1* (Academic Press, 1974)

This is the most readable of the many books written on the theoretical background and major debates of this period. There are excellent chapters on the medieval background, the rise of the state and the emergence of capitalism.

Sources on Tudor Economy and Society

Many books contain primary extracts and there is a variety of accessible published primary sources covering the Tudor period as a whole or in parts.

> **H.E.S. Fisher and A.R.J. Jurica,** *Documents in English Economic History from 1000–1760* (Bell and Sons, 1977)

This is now the standard source for economic documents.

> **R.H. Tawney and E. Power (eds.),** *Tudor Economic Documents* (3 volumes; London, 1924)

> **A.E. Bland et al (eds.),** *English Economic History, Select Documents* (G. Bell and Sons, 1914)

Apart from a very wide range of economic documents these books contain a good selection of social material, particularly on poverty.

> **J.M. Jack,** *Trade and Industry in Tudor and Stuart England* (George Allen and Unwin, 1977)

As well as providing some interesting alternative economic documents, this seminar book contains useful sections on economic theory and interpretation.

Acknowledgements

The publishers would like to thank the following for permission to reproduce copyright illustrations:

Cover – Detail from 'The Life and Death of Sir Henry Unton', artist unknown, c. 1596, National Portrait Gallery, London. The Mansell Collection p. 131. Crown Copyright, Historic Royal Palaces p. 144 top. Reproduced by Permission of the Syndics of the Fitzwilliam Museum, Cambridge p. 144 lower. Royal Commission on the Historical Monuments of England p. 145 top © The National Trust, 1992 p. 145 lower. Royal Collection, St James's Palace © 1992 Her Majesty The Queen p. 148.

The publishers would like to thank the following for permission to reproduce material in this volume:

Martin Secker and Warburg Ltd for the extract from *The Lisle Letters*, M. St Clare Byrne ed., (1985); Thames and Hudson Ltd for the extracts from *The Diary of Baron Waldstein: A Traveller in Elizabethan England*, G. W. Groos (trans), (1981).

Every effort has been made to trace and acknowledge ownership of copyright. The publishers will be glad to make suitable arrangements with any copyright holders whom it has not been possible to contact.

Index